RUNNING
LIGHT

SUN, SAND &
THE PSYCHOLOGICAL PREPARATION
FOR THE TOUGHEST FOOTRACE ON EARTH

Craig Williams

ISBN: 978-1-78808-544-1 (print)
ISBN: 978-1-78808-545-8 (ebook)

ABOUT THE AUTHOR

Craig Williams left the Royal Marines in 2008 and unable to adjust to civilian life spent a period homeless, penniless and jobless. Craig now coaches people to be better in all aspects of their lives including food, fitness, lifestyle and business. Craig is an author, active public speaker, fitness entrepreneur, television extreme weight loss consultant and marketing coach. Craig lives in Shropshire along with wife Paula and two sons Danny & Matthew.

Connect with Craig and get all the resources and additional resources at RunningLightBook. com

DEDICATION

My wife Paula & two sons Danny & Matthew

THANK YOU

I would like to extend a heartfelt thank you to the following people who have made my MDS journey and this possible.

As always, the backbone of everything I am and do is my wife Paula and sons Danny & Matty. Thank you for the many sacrifices you made for me to chase a dream... then spend way too long writing about it.

Thanks Dad for sorting my food and acting as chief communications officer throughout the race. Thanks to my brother Joe for being my most honest critic at times, but ultimately helping me finalise this book.

The whole TEAM Bootcamp community especially the staff, Elinor Evans who gave me the little nudge I needed and Mark Smyth... business partner, friend and fellow MDS runner.

The Walking With the Wounded team plus all my family and friends that sponsored me especially Harriet Christian, the Pilkington Trust and Siobhan Hicks.

Thank you to all the contributors to this book including friends and mentors Phil Kelly & Phil Quirk. Thanks confidante and advisor Tony

Sheridan and the pure gentlemen who I had the privilege of sharing Tent 115 with including Pete Godbehere, Simon Harris, Euan Eltringham, Paul Hammond, Mark Woodall & Mark, who helped me through each day.

Special mention to my comrades of the world's first and finest, all gentlemen's club, the Camel Club. You were and always will be a constant source of wit, banter and completely inappropriate social media posts.

CONTENTS

Chapter 1
Origins Of A Reluctant Runner 1

Chapter 2
How To Use This Book 13

Chapter 3
The Journey 23

Chapter 4
Mindset (Estimated 60% Of Your Mds Success) 29

Chapter 5
Motivation 39

Chapter 6
Biggest Fears Am I Enough??? 51

Chapter 7
I Am Worried I'm Not Fit Enough... What Does Fit
Enough Look Like To You? 57

Chapter 8
What Do You Expect? 81

Chapter 9
Race Day Mindset 89

Chapter 10
What If I Get Injured? 105

Chapter 11
The B Word 117

Chapter 12
Fitness (Estimated 20% Of Your Mds Success) 127

Chapter 13
Food (Estimated 10% Of Your Mds Success) 153

Chapter 14
Kit (Estimated 10% Of Your Mds Success) 167

Chapter 15
Weight 175

Chapter 16
Before You Go 187

Chapter 17
From The Experts & Past Runners 191

Chapter 18
Interview With Tony Sheridan 201

Chapter 19
Interview With Phil Kelly 225

Chapter 20
My Race Diary 251

CHAPTER 1

ORIGINS OF
A RELUCTANT RUNNER

'Run when your body doesn't want to!'

James Cracknell
(when asked about his
training for the MDS)

I suppose I could start with the big story about my life to date, where I was born and what it was like growing up but I'll save that for another book someday. I want to talk about my journey to and through the toughest footrace on Earth despite not really considering myself a runner. I'm not sure where you see yourself on the running spectrum. You have obviously got an interest in running and taking part in stupid events such as the Marathon des Sables (MDS) or you wouldn't be reading this book. Personally, I wouldn't class myself as an avid, consistent runner. I ran a bit when I was growing up. A bit with school, a little bit from the police, some more in the race riots Yorkshire back in the day but not a great deal. I squeezed myself onto the cross-country team in high school, I think someone was ill or something, but I was always too heavy to be a decent kind of runner. No, wait... delete heavy and insert fat!

My identity at school was 'the poor chubby kid with the ginger afro, the one that's not a bad runner for a fat kid.' In my late teens, I managed to slip through the Royal Marines recruitment net and obviously, I had a fair bit of running to do then but I still wasn't a fantastic runner. In fact, my identity then changed to 'the chubby ginger marine that is shit at pull ups, but can (surprisingly) run!' Maybe I would have been better if I had enjoyed it more but it always seemed like a punishment. Looking back, I quite liked being a bit of a stealth runner... but not as much as I enjoyed being an eating and boozing machine. There was nothing 'stealth' about that!

To make things worse I had some very noticeable physiological issues too. First, I've got incredibly flat feet. In a tux and bare feet, I could be mistaken for a penguin especially with my unique waddle. The short musculature in the back of my legs causes me to walk on my toes and meant I was plagued with Achilles issues and blisters throughout my service. You wouldn't think having size 10 legs with size 5 hamstrings and calves would be too much of an issue, but you would change your mind after a few miles of foot slapping your way along miles of country road in military boots carrying a house on your back. Probably a little fed up of having to stomach the sight of my bruised, battered and blistered flippers every week, my medical officer referred me to a bio-mechanic.

After an initial assessment and about 45 minutes of teeth sucking, he said "Craig if you were a horse… we'd put you down! You've got one shoulder excessively lower than the other, one arm longer than the other, all the muscles in the back of your legs are way too short and as tight as piano strings, and you have the flattest feet that I have seen in 20 years of doing this job. Oh, and some funky tropical fungal infection in your toenails that you're probably going to have for the rest of your life!" 'And the bad news?' I thought. I'm sure he said '…and you're ginger!' under his breath too, but I will never be sure.

The bio-mechanic made some specialist insoles for my boots which I ditched during an exercise in the arctic. They had the cold retention properties of an Inuit fridge and caused frost nip on my feet at minus 13.

I have a terrible history of horrific blisters. It stems from my odd shaped plates of meat never really fitting the 'average foot' mould. Imagine trying to stuff Action Man's flipper into Barbie's espadrilles and you get the idea! So that was just my physiology, I was far from a finely tuned athlete, but who was I to let something like physics and biology dictate what I would do?

So how did I end up running the MDS?

Deep breath. This gets personal from here and I haven't shared this with the masses before. If it gets too emotional give me some space. When I left the Marines, my head was a bit messed up. Erm... no, in fact, it was very messed up. I think the technical terms could be 'bat shit mental' and 'fucked up crazy'! Shocking that I couldn't function in civilian life, I mean it was only 12 years of systematic conditioning to kill the enemy and defend the realm?! Joking aside, I was really struggling. If I had possessed the balls to leave my mum and young son alone on this planet, I wouldn't be here right now. Even simple tasks like opening a bank account and using the phone seemed impossible. At the time, I wasn't living I was wallowing in suicidal depression and guilt. I'll skip the usual expressive writing to hammer home the point. Just accept I was fucked up!

Getting out in the fresh air helped clear my mind a little and I found the sound of the local river was very calming. There's something strangely therapeutic about listening to sanitary towels flapping in the current caught in the prongs of a rusty Asda trolley. One of the hardest things was my closest friends and family constantly trying to 'talk' me through it. After exhausting every avoidance technique possible I started to jog as a way of being alone. It stopped people trying to talk to me. I know it sounds anti-social, but I wasn't ready for talking things through. They'd be like, "Craig, I know you're suffering right now but you should try talking about blah blah". They never actually said blah blah, that was the point I zoned out and drifted back to the '7 ways to dispatch an enemy sentry with a Commando dagger' (AKA '7 ways to silence a probing friend with an everyday item'). Strange, but I found that fewer people were as willing to quiz me about Afghan and Iraq when I was running. Eventually, it would be counselling that would help me get back on my (world's flattest) feet, but at that point I wasn't ready and just needed to be alone. Running did that.

Around the same time, I got a rescue dog called Earl. He was the most stubborn English Bull Terrier you've ever met. My partner at the time got him as a companion and I liked him instantly because his white fur and jet black markings around his face made him look like a Storm Trooper. Sadly, Earl would be put to sleep a year later when we worked out Great White Shark and Diamondback rattler were in his bloodline, but before he caused significant changes in my psychological state. Right now, you maybe be thinking that Earl was one of these super sensitive disability dogs that fry eggs for the blind or sense when an autistic boy needs a shit, but he wasn't. He had the emotional intelligence of a flip-flop and had the narcissistic traits of Hannibal Lecter. He had no training… as in zero… nothing what so ever. He did what he wanted when he wanted and had a look in his big black storm trooper eyes that said, 'What's your fucking problem Ginge?'

He had this routine. I'd be sat in the chair (he allowed me 1 hour of chair time a day!), festering in my own self-hatred and depression. Hauling my ass outside was at the very bottom of my to-do list under 'don't forget to change my undies' and 'hate the world' and this big daft dog would basically jump up onto the back of the chair and lick and chew my ear relentlessly. It was his signal that he wanted to go for a walk. I would try fighting him off, but remember how the stupid kid at school was always so much stronger than everyone else? I was no match for his strength. There were times when I would go nuts but Earl was just relentless. He knew I would eventually give in and with the same 'What's your fucking problem Ginge?' look in his eyes, I would grab a handful of poo bags, attach the lead to his collar and take him out.

Nightmare... but that was just the preliminary stage. Stage 2... 'full-on twat' mode started the minute we got outside. With the torque of a thousand glaciers, he would drag me to the park and as I let him off the straining leash the little terrorizing bastard would sprint off like a rocket assisted greyhound! I would be like 'No Earl, please... not again!' He would dash along a pathway at the side of the river, but not before he retrieved his favourite stick on the way. I say stick, I mean chewed up, saliva clad limb from the lower tier of a giant Sequoia! He shared this thing with the BFG who used it as a walking stick. He would gallop along with his stick, cracking the shins of anybody unfortunate enough to get in the way. He'd run alongside the river for about a mile and a half, over a footbridge, down the other side and I would have to sprint after him. I tried to keep up, but I'm not sure Haile Gebrselassie had the capacity to pace Earl and I didn't stand a chance having to stop every 50 yards to apologise to the hopping grandads rubbing their bruised shins with an angry look on their faces. He just ran and ran. He wouldn't stop until he got to a huge pool in the river near my home where he would jump in and swim laps for what seemed like an age. It didn't matter what the weather was, bright summer sun to frosty winters day, nothing would perturb him from his doggy duathlon two or three times a day. He forced me to run. I'd almost collapse after my 3-mile sprint and desperately needed the rest on the bank near the pool while the dickhead paddled circles in the currents.

Though I didn't know it at the time, Earl did two things. First, he got me running consistently. I was running three miles two or three times a day, every day. Secondly, he forced me to sit and watch him swim. I won't lie, there were times when I would be like, "That's it! I'm not waiting here any longer!" and wade in to drag him out. Often though, I would just sit and let my mind wander. I would think about... well, stuff! During that thinking time, I was getting fresh air, the noise of the water was really comforting and that became the beginning of me sorting my shit out. It gave me time to work out how I felt about things I saw and did in the Marines as well as other aspects of life before. I have a lot to thank 'Earl the Bastard' for, but he really was a cock at times!

So that's how I started running. It became my coping strategy and part of my new identity. I developed an interest in more fitness and I found that, contrary to fitness in the Marines, it no longer felt like a punishment. I suddenly enjoyed. Looking back, I thought I had developed a love of running but on reflection, I actually loved what running developed in me. I loved getting out in the fresh air, clearing my head and I loved the feeling afterwards. My wife Paula taught me Mindfulness, it's very popular nowadays and running put me into a mindful state. It changed my mental state from 'mind full' to 'mindful' which eradicated stress and gave me the headspace to untangle the shitty mess of thoughts I had about war, conflict, guilt and life in general.

For a long time, I had harboured the dream of completing the Marathon Des Sables. The slogan of 'The Toughest Footrace on Earth' was the biggest draw for me and it was high on my bucket list just behind 'Develop cattle prod for unruly canines'... and 'have naked twister competition with Ellie Goulding and an industrial sized tub of Swarfega'. I'd seen video clips and read articles about it and was further inspired by James Cracknell's documentary about the race on the Discovery Channel. I set a goal of finishing the MDS before I was forty. Time was running out. If I didn't tackle this now I'm going to miss the boat. We all love deadlines, we love the way deadlines sound when they fly past us.

I applied through the ballet in 2014 & 2015, but heard nothing. I was rapidly approaching forty and thought 'now is the time'. In 2016, I applied again and once again missed out in the public ballet. In 2017 I was to be forty… it had to happen now! I immediately wrote to service charity Walking With The Wounded (WWTW) begging for a place. Thankfully Vicks, who manages the events for WWTW, gave me a place on the team. Following my journey from fecked up veteran to semi-ok civilian, it felt right that I should be part of the WWTW team. Fittingly the money I raised would be going to their new initiative Head Start which will help similar struggling veterans resettle and find work while getting their heads in order. Strangely they rejected my idea of giving every PTSD sufferer a whack job bull terrier!

It seemed a big jump from flailing three miles through the park chasing a tree wielding English Bull Terroriser to running across the Sahara, but is it a big jump? … really? I mean the distance, the heat and all that are very different but it's just what the human body is designed for. We evolved to run and even me with my little penguin feet and piano tight hamstrings & calves are designed for running.

During a talk that Dr. Mike Stroud (Author of Survival of The Fittest) gave during the MDS expo, he presented the idea we were not the hunter gathers we first thought. The idea of the men heading out and gathering berries and bark and insects may well be a myth. In fact, it is very likely that we were persistence hunters. We would run our prey into the ground. We have developed the ability to dissipate heat incredibly well. It didn't feel that way in the middle of the midday Sahara sun as my brain roasted, but compared to many animals we can run and run and run because we regulate temperature well. Deer, for example, would need to stop and pant to dissipate heat.

So, we're born to run. In my role as a mindset coach, I have come to accept that most humans mistakenly think that everything is against them when it comes to running. Conversely, everything in nature is working for us. Let us use the analogy of a Land Rover.

Land Rovers are exceptional at what they have been designed for. They can cross the toughest terrain in all weathers and the powerful diesel engine just keeps on trucking. You're a Land Rover... and if we leave a Land Rover to stand for a few years it doesn't stop being a Land Rover. Ok, the brakes may seize up, the fluids spoil and the tyres and suspension may perish, but it's still a Land Rover.

Don't think, just because you've stood dormant for a while or that you're carrying a little extra weight or do lots of regularly running, that things are stacked against you. They're not, nature is there for you, it has your back. In this book, I am going to explain how I dragged my stagnant Land Rover ass out of the garage. Changed the fluids, replaced the tyres, checked the engine and running gear and once I had run a few MOT checks I was more than physically capable of cracking the MDS and so will you.

The only thing that is going to get in the way is the top 6 inches of your body. The grey matter between your ears and the minute electrical impulses bouncing around your brain. That's what this book is about, I want you to know and believe that even if you've got six weeks left to go before any race you have all the time and resources you need. You can get through this regardless of your fitness ability, all that's going to let you down is your mindset. Don't listen to the so-called running experts that generate business by evoking fear in the average runner. Your conscious and subconscious mind controls every-thing. There's a saying in the Marines "when your body gives in, your head takes over and when your head gives in... your heart takes over". In this book, we're going to wire all this up. We're going to identify what aspects of your thoughts, beliefs and emotions you can recruit to keep you going in the darkest times in the Sahara or any other stupid event you have planned. We're going to develop a deep-rooted desire in your heart that refuses to give in. We will call on every resource you possess to get you through this because you know what's coming at the end! At the end, you will cry with a mix of relief and unrivalled pride. Like me and every other person that has finished this race before you... you're going to know that you've done something incredibly special. Something that very few people in the world could even comprehend. They have no idea what the human body can get through but you will know. You will have touched exhaustion, heat illness, diced with severe dehydration and endured pain to an extent that the body turns it off to protect you! You will know you have truly tested yourself, pushed yourself to the limits and you can stand tall, proud in the fact that you are a member of a very small community of elite people in this world. Regardless of your finish time or position, even if you limp, crawl or have to be dragged over the finish line, you will have the medal. Just like earning a green beret in the Royal Marines, it doesn't matter if you're the top recruit or slip through the net, you get the green beret and everybody looks at you the same. You get the same reception when you return and your actions demand the same respect as everyone that wears the finisher's t-shirt and medal.

So that's what this book is about.

CHAPTER 2

HOW TO
USE THIS BOOK

'Go for it now… The future is promised to no one'

Originally by **Wayne Dyer**,
shared by **Elisabet Barnes**
at the MDS Expo

This chapter is meant to be a little bit of 'Why you should pay attention to me' and a healthy spoonful of 'here's the tangible shit it's built on'. You can either read it now or dive straight into the other chapters and read it later, but you should know that there is theory behind this book. There are two ways I could have written this section. Route A, the most traditional route, where I write all about my academic qualifications and ultra-running experience (possibly the best 100 words you have ever read *wink*) and how I've consulted on TV, helped thousands improve their health, fitness and life. I opted for route B where I outline how each of the following topics came about and continue the same writing style from chapter 1. I'm sure some of you would have preferred route A, but this book is different. Predominantly we are talking about creating new thoughts, beliefs and emotions within your conscious and subconscious mind and there lies the problem.

Our beliefs are created throughout life, often forged before the age of 7 though many change throughout life. Take your age for example. There was a time in your life when you believed you were 7 years old. You know that it is no longer true. Santa is another example. There's living proof your mum and dad lie to you! We believe that our parent has our best interest at heart and they would never do anything that might hurt us, but often your parents or certainly the significant adults in your life install small programmes in your mind for protection. They are for your own good in many cases, but can hold you back and smother your achievements. 'Don't do that, it's dangerous!'. My mum even told me I was the ugliest baby she had ever seen. No wonder I never pursued a career as a Men's Health cover model!

Anyway, these beliefs along with your values, decisions, memories and meta programmes all act as a filter and govern everything we do. Even when you think you are acting consciously, you are being subconsciously steered.

Later in this book, I will explain the function of the Critical Faculty (CF). The CF acts like a border guard controlling a gateway from your conscious to your subconscious mind and it's selective on what it allows through.

Picture this... Despite my ginger afro, I always looked way older than I was. I have looked about 35 since I was 16 so I was always the one that had to speak to the bouncers when we tried to enter night clubs under age. You probably know the drill...

'Hang on there fellas' the bouncer would say. 'How old are you?'

'18...' I would say trying to sound older (however that works?)

'Not tonight lads!' - Rejected!

Just like the facts and figures hitting your CF we just could not get through. So, what's the answer... Well, we need a better reply... a story to bypass the bouncers' routine of:

Thoughts: these lads look under age - They tell me their age...

Beliefs: based on my experience I don't believe them...

Emotions: Based on the school kids that I let in last week that went on a 4-person mission to rid the world of Jaeger Bombs and got so pissed they nearly cost me my job, I'm not taking any chances...

Actions: Go eat pick-a-mix in the cinema, you wankers!

So, stories are the way to bypass the CF. Like Red Indian chiefs passing on generations of experience around a campfire at night. Stories cause us to reflect and help new thoughts, beliefs and emotions to seep into the subconscious mind.

So, there is a reason for the light-hearted approach and the self-deprecating humour in this book.

Great story... but seriously what is all this based on?

I knew during my preparation that the mind was the single most important 'tool' I needed to get right. I would read through some of the posts in the Facebook group about what food would give you the edge and what kit would dramatically increase your chances of success. I saw huge threads with hundreds of comments about how to shave 3 grams from your left insole and why you should have your wisdom teeth and appendix surgically removed to ensure you were as light as possible and I thought 'Wow... these guys have it so wrong!' Hear me out, the weight of your pack is incredibly important and is a huge factor in your success across the Sahara, but here's my theory.

Two Pack Theory

I believe everyone takes two packs into the desert. One pack is your physical pack. It holds all your kit, equipment, food and water. The physical pack is the one 99% of MDS runners obsess about, but there is another pack. A psychological pack that we carry in or mind. This pack is metaphorical and contains your deepest fears, worries, self-doubt, thoughts, beliefs, and emotions that all of which can crush you! This pack far outweighs your physical bag and can stop you in your tracks if left unchecked.

I arrived in the Sahara woefully under prepared physically. Life had got in the way and I didn't have the time to train how I had intended when I first signed up for the event some 16 months prior. In fact, 3 weeks from the race I went for my last long run and barely made 20 miles before I had to call my wife to come and collect me. During the MDS, I ran the first stage over horrendous sand dunes and collapsed into the medical tent at checkpoint 1. I had to fend off the Doc Trotters who could see I was in distress through heat illness and fatigue to avoid a time penalty. After 9km of undulating sand dunes and constant head on sandstorms the Sahara put me over its knee and slapped my arse like I was a petulant child! Later I would discover that more people left the race that day than in the entire event any year before. ...and in my mind, I kept thinking... 'This desert has played right into my hands!'

To get great answers, we first need to ask great questions. Here's the first... What the hell have you done to prepare your mind for this?

If you're annoyed or aggravated, beating yourself up or beating yourself down, confused or complexed, distraught or demotivated... the answer is probably 'Nothing!'

That's great, we can get started there and the only way is up.

The good news is that when you follow the strategies outlined in this book, you too will believe the desert has played right into your hands. You will see obstacles and issues not as obstacles that are 'in the way', but as things that are 'along the way'. All art of the journey and each one we can work through and accept as being of the process of earning an MDS finishers medal.

A word of warning... That doesn't mean you should forget all physical training, far from it. A huge part of the mindset stuff is respecting the desert and the conditions that it will throw at you. Only fools leave it to chance. Having operated in every environment throughout the world from the frozen arctic to the hot humid festering jungle I can tell you that the desert is the most inhospitable environment you could face! The desert is a barren expanse of deadly terrain. It's a bit like living in Texas. A very good friend of mine Chris Stockdale emigrated to Texas after leaving the Marines. We talk regularly and I asked him what living in Texas was like. He told me how rattlesnakes lived in an abundance around his ranch and I was like 'Holy fuck, people must get bitten all the time!' 'Not really' He said. 'We just give them a little space and we all get along just fine'. It's just like the MDS. The rattlesnake has the speed and potency to kill you or certainly make life a little unpleasant. If you give it a little space and respect the fact that it's a tough little hombre, you'll be fine. The minute you start to piss it off, fight it or work against it and you are going to get bitten... hard!

So, apart from horrendous grammar and terrible spelling this book has been written differently to most running books. Like business, most people create some crazy widget or product thinking they have a million-dollar idea. They invest thousands into bringing their idea or product into reality and then struggle to find an audience to sell it to. I did the opposite and asked you what should appear in these pages.

Each of the following sections arose after a short survey that I did in the 2016 MDS runners group on Facebook. I asked the following questions:

1. What is your biggest challenge regarding your preparation for the MDS?
2. What is your goal for the MDS?
   - A - Compete,
   - B - Top 500,
   - C - Top 1000,
   - D - Just complete the feckin' thing!
3. What are your 2 biggest fears right now?

Some of the answers inspired me and others astounded me, but overall, the survey was very interesting and matched my own thoughts, beliefs, and feelings. I sorted the results by frequency and condensed them into the topics that make up the following sections;

1. Mindset
2. Fitness
3. Food
4. Kit

Once complete, I set about interviewing as many topic-specific experts that I had within my network. From polar explorers to previous runners (and walkers) of the MDS to Olympic performance coaches and much more. I have also included much of my own tips, techniques, and strategies developed throughout my coaching. I, along with my wife Paula and our amazing team, help thousands of people each year to think, eat & move better. Clients come to us with a wide range of issues from food addiction and chronic stress to extreme obesity and diabetes. Paula and I help them all with a blend of coaching techniques including Neuro Linguistic Programming (NLP), hypnotherapy, and mindfulness along with smart functional fitness training and conditioning delivered in a no-compromise manner. We do whatever it takes to enable people to change their lives and to be better.

So here goes, but before we get started remember to check out the supporting resources and additional lessons at RunningLightBook. com/Resources. I will update videos and inter-views and downloadable resources regularly. I will refer to the extra videos, cheat sheets and audio files throughout this book and only ask that you maintain its integrity. The extra resource area is only for people that have purchased this book and should not be shared freely.

CHAPTER 3

THE **JOURNEY**

'Remember where you are... and that it will end!'

James Cracknell

My legs were throbbing and my tent mates gasped as I peeled a blood-soaked sock from my tired and battered feet. I was desperate to replace as much of the energy I had expelled during today's stage of the MDS and a small pot of water sat upon a makeshift stove buried in the desert sand shielded from the sandstorm by my aching body. I gasped as my sock broke free from the dried blood on my large toe taking some of the skin with it. I wriggled a little with the pain and paused for a second to let the pain ease. I compressed my foot and as I grit my teeth I caught site of a tiny pocket of air spring free from the base of the cooking pot and bubble up to the surface.

I'm not sure if it was the hunger, the fatigue or the pain that obscured my thinking, but I found myself thinking about the water boiling. I was amazed how water boiling doesn't happen instantly. It comes from a steady increase of temperature. A single bubble doesn't make a pot boil, but many tiny bubbles do. A single word doesn't make a book. A single step does not make an ultra-run.

This book is a bubbling pot of tiny tips and tricks that together will create an unshakeable confidence in your ability, a clear strategy to prepare for the toughest footrace on earth and a boiling pot of great energy, motivation and inspiration.

I want to offer you a 'picture' to ensure you read the whole of this book and implement the strategies outlined. An exciting future version of you to pull you through the tough times during your preparation. The picture is a new image of you. A renewed refined and improved self-image of yourself. I promise that after reading this book you will think differently, train differently and as many of the tricks and techniques are transferable to other aspects of life, you will live differently.

It sounds like a big claim but imagine the pot of water boiling. I recommend you concentrate on creating one bubble at a time, knowing they will soon add up and will change you to a boiling pot of energy! What you have signed up for here is a big challenge, but every challenge is a journey and every journey is a series of small steps.

Through these small steps, you will develop the ability to tap into unknown potential deep in both your conscious and subconscious mind and have your thoughts, beliefs and emotions work for you. Not against you.

I pleaded with one runner not to throw in the towel as we roped up one of the largest sand dunes along the MDS route. In a calm and collected manner, he stood, turned and with the immortal words "I'm done" started walking back down to the checkpoint below. I rapidly went through every approach possible to try and get him to stay with it. I tried a nice, friendly approach, a logical approach and as he got further I even tried the personal insult approach. I stopped short of the 'your mama' jokes! Nothing worked. His head had gone. He was enjoying the momentary relief of not having to do another step in the desert, unfortunately, that relief doesn't last forever and soon after it is replaced with the thoughts and feelings you get with failure. The feelings that seem to crush your heart and tie knots in your stomach. He truly was done and for hours after I watched he slope off down the sand dune, I questioned what went wrong. He was fitter, faster and more experienced than me. He just didn't have his head straight.

So, like a boxer outsmarting and psyching out a stronger and faster opponent, you will mould the mind of a winner. You will develop a comforting knowledge in your own abilities, knowing that only unforeseen circumstances and not doing what you now know can stop you from completing the MDS.

Now I cannot make you the fittest person in the world and we all have a natural born ability. Reading this book will certainly not enable you to run the fastest in the world, but it will help you run the fastest MDS possible for you.

In this chapter, we have explored how every challenge is a journey and every journey is a series of small steps. You may well be overwhelmed at the minute which can be paralysing, but it doesn't have to be that way. You may recognise all the different ways you are overwhelmed by the MDS... but... people change and you're a person, so you can change too. In the next few chapters we will look at creating a powerful picture of you in the future that can pull you through the tough training and the incredible challenge you have.

PART 1

CHAPTER 4

MINDSET
(ESTIMATED 60% OF YOUR MDS SUCCESS)

Two Wolves Within

A Cherokee Indian is talking with his grandson and he says there are two wolves inside of us which are always at war with each other.

One of them is a good wolf which represents things like kindness, bravery and love. The other is a bad wolf, which represents things like greed, hatred and fear.

The grandson stops and thinks about it for a second then he looks up at his grandfather and says, "Grandfather, which one wins?"

The grandfather quietly replies, the one you feed

I n this section, I want to explain what I mean by mindset. Lots of people talk a lot about mindset and it comes along with other words such as mindfulness and meditation and stuff... but what I mean by mindset is... when you are out in the desert running with no one else around you or even sat in your tent at night you never really alone. You see there is always another voice that you can hear. The other voice is your internal dialogue and most people's internal dialogue works against them. It works to protect you and keep you safe. It will highlight the potential dangers and problems that your brain identifies. It stops you from embarrassing, humiliating or hurting yourself. It has been created through a history of embarrassing and humiliating moments through life along with lessons our parents and other significant adults have taught us. Even stories we come across in the media can cement deep rooted beliefs and thought processes in our mind geared towards 'protection'.

The thing is, when you're going to run across the Sahara or whenever you are going to attempt an event that is a challenge that most people would steer away from because of the risk or failure and because of potential harm, we need the opposite. We need a different internal dialogue that will help, encourage and motivate us. One that will help us believe in ourselves not second guess our abilities. We need a reliable friend and ally.

So, when I talk about mindset, I am talking about changing the words we say to ourselves through that inner voice. We want words that will motivate and inspire us. An internal dialogue that reminds us of our goals, our motivation to do these crazy events and the consequences if we don't. We don't want words that will keep us safe and secure and comfortable. We need words to excite us. I am a huge believer that things come way too easy for us nowadays but that isn't how we became apex predators took over the world. Life isn't the challenge it used to be. Most people chase comfort thinking that the right money, right home, right car and right clothes will bring happiness, but comfort is not what humans truly need. Comfort breeds mediocrity and I would argue that humans need the challenge to create excitement and excitement pull us through life. It will make our lives bigger than we could ever believe and that's not just excitement for you. It's not a selfish thing. You see, whenever we light the way for others around us we inspire them to do more and take on more challenges. One of the biggest driving forces for me was the ability to take my story about the MDS and, through this book and the talks that I have created around it, encourage others to change their internal dialogue, break free of the norm and chase their dreams.

I think you probably already agree with this if you have signed up for the MDS or have done other daft events in the past. In fact, you are probably not doing the MDS because you are a good runner and it's a natural progression. There is probably some other deeper reason. Even if you are a good runner there is probably another reason why you signed up. Maybe you want to stand out amongst the group of runners you move in? See after this event you are no longer another runner doing the 5k's, 10k's, marathons and ultra's, you are a finisher of the toughest footrace on earth.

You are at the top of your group. The one that dared and others will come up with excuses and all the reasons under the sun about why they haven't done it. "...it's too expensive', `...it's not the hardest' blah blah blah... well compared to their cheap talk, it is expensive and my mindset allowed me to complete the race with no personal outlay of money so what's there excuse now?

Think about this. Our world has not been created by the comfortable ones that went with the flow or refused to rock the boat, but by the pure head-the-balls that dared to dream. The people that have gone out on a limb, the people that went against their internal dialogue and went against the things that others around them are saying that have shaped our world.

Mindset isn't about fluffy pictures or clouds and bouncing lambs that make you feel safe and comfortable, it's about recruiting your mind as the greatest ally, your partner in crime, the other half of the dynamic duo that's going to get you through the desert. Now it all sounds tough because some of these habits and the things you say to yourself are ingrained and deep in your values and beliefs, but people change and you're a person so you can change too!

Your new mindset won't just help you during the event either, but before in your preparation and long after the race.

You can change all the beliefs you have, the small insecure voice in your head can become the mother frikkin apex predator you were meant to be. You can alter your self-image of who you are, where you belong in life and in your family group and what you are going to do in your future.

A few years back I was pretty broken. I could not have been any lower in life. I was homeless, penniless, didn't have a job and I felt I had very few options. I had two sons that I didn't have any access to and at times I felt I had nothing. Looking back now, I know that is not true. I did have something. I had a deep-rooted desire to be more. I really believe this is where it all started for me with the mindset things because deep down I knew I could be more. Some kind of seed was growing inside me saying 'You are going to be more than this, you are going to DO more than this and you are going to leave a legacy on this world'. I believe I will leave this world with gifts from my experiences along my journey and so will you, but you have to go get them. The MDS for me was another big step in becoming someone that inspires others. Another big step in gaining knowledge and a deep understanding of myself and how my mind functions. One more step in my ability to be honest with myself about my worries, fears and understanding the things I would say to myself during periods of pain and fatigue.

Looking back, my mindset was very negative. I was actually quite fearful of my fear full internal dialogue. Now I have a completely different outlook about everything I do. I would be lying if I said it was 100% all the time, because sometimes your old habits and thought patterns creep in, but consistently it is much better. You never really lose your mental fears and worries. They are always there, but we can learn to fly above them, challenge them and look for evidence to dispel them rather than support them. Consistently my mindset is a positive one. Consistently my mindset looks for ways to zag when everyone else is zigging and don't want to follow the masses that are comfortable anymore, I want to be in the top 0.001% of people that have completed the toughest footrace on earth. This book will give you the very best chance of that.

Here's a pretty simple equation. Full fitness X ½ a mindset is weaker than a full mindset with ½ your fitness.

With the right mindset, it is incredible what you can do. Flying back from Morocco after the MDS I sat next to a lady called Rebecca who completed the MDS despite having very little running experience. In fact, she pretty much walked the whole way. Don't be so arrogant to think that walking the MDS is easy. Having been there I wouldn't want to be exposed to the elements as much as the back markers are. Their time and resources to recover from the day and prepare for the next are dramatically reduced and they spend a considerably greater amount of time alone with their internal dialogue than the elite and mid-pack runners do. I asked Rebecca how she had completed the race when others, even the guy with over 100 Ironman races under his belt couldn't. Her answer was insightful. "The only way I was coming out of that desert was with a finishers medal around my neck or in a body bag". Let's look at what is not being said. Rebecca's statement suggests she went to the desert not really thinking about 'if' she could do it, but how she 'will' do it. She assumed she would finish and she was 100% committed. Regardless of how high the sand dunes, how hot the blowing winds and how sore her feet would become, she was going to take every little step required to complete it.

So, this is what I am talking about with regards to mindset. Now I don't know where you are with your preparation for the MDS, I don't know what your aspirations are. I'm not sure if they are realistic, unrealistic or whatever, but one thing I do know is that your internal dialogue is going to be with you every step of the way. Every time you climb a large sand, dune burst a blister, wipe sweat from your brow, every time you adjust your pack because it is hurting your internal dialogue is going to be whispering in your ear. It won't be holding back either. It will be blunt and to the point, because nobody else can hear it. If we said the things we say to ourselves in private to another person in public they would punch us in the face!!! Such is the gravity and nastiness of the things we say through our internal dialogue. You need to know that your internal dialogue is working for you, not against you and it's easy said than done. At times, it can be very tough. Especially when your willpower is low and all the signs and signals your senses are receiving are screaming STOP... be safe... find comfort! However, with practice and by implementing a few strategies from this book, you can alter the way in which you talk to yourself.

You can do this.

I 100% believe that every human being was designed for this shit. We only have to look at our anatomy to know we are built to run and cover large distances. We originate from people that thought nothing of walking from Africa to Europe because the rains didn't come or the wildebeest buggered off. You can be the one on the aeroplane with the finishers medal. I slept with mine for a week after the event and that can be you. You could have the t-shirt and the awkward conversations with people that don't even know the race exists. You can also be the one, like me, that uses their story to motivate and inspire others.

Whatever it is, we want to change your internal dialogue from the bully who wants to keep you safe and secure. We want to kick the fuck out of that and grab life by the horns. We want to be something. We want to be a finisher of the toughest footrace on earth.

In this chapter, we have explored how your internal dialogue will be with you through the whole of the MDS and it will either help you or crush you. You may have already been affected by your negative subconscious personal chatter, but it doesn't have to be that way. You may recognise all the different ways you are talking yourself out of training, or talking yourself into failure... *but*... people change and you're a person, so you can change too. In the next few chapters we will look at changing the words we use to excite us to do this!!! Against all the current odds.

CHAPTER 5

MOTIVATION

'Remember what others have sacrificed for you to be here?'
James Cracknell

H aving discussed mindset in the previous chapter, the next logical step is defining your motivation. What is your big reason why? Do you have a reason why? To illustrate the point, think about this. If I laid a long plank of wood along the floor and I asked you walk along it, would you? Yes... But what if the plank was elevated between two skyscrapers and was hundreds of feet from the ground? Most definitely no! The reason you are now reluctant is because the consequences are much higher when the plank spans two tall buildings. We no longer worry about looking like a fool if we cannot keep our balance, getting it wrong now means certain death!

We lack motivation when our reason 'why' is smaller or less powerful than the consequences of failure (or even sometimes success). Imagine now that you are stood at the top of one of the towers and the plank is stretched out in front of you spanning the gap to the second tower. The second building is on fire and is burning rapidly, and your child is calling you from one of the rooms. Your child is doomed with no way of escaping unless you cross the plank and rescue her. Would you cross? Personally, I wouldn't even question it. My desire to save my child would be too great.

So, what is your big reason why? Have you spent time thinking about it? Maybe it is super clear in your mind already and if not, and you struggle to think of your reason why... imagine if you could... what might it be?

For me I wanted the test. I wanted to know if I could complete it and I also wanted to be able to use my experience to help inspire and motivate others. My big goal in life is to help other people be better than they were yesterday. I believe though somethings can be learnt through books or college programmes, other things must be experienced and witnessed first-hand. The MDS for me was to be a reset for my busy professional life, but more importantly a very personal insight into my own abilities, my inner most thoughts, fears and strength, a short sharp test of my resolve and the ability to use those lessons to help others in the future. All those things aligned with my highest values in life and ultimately your highest values will dictate what you do.

With an event like the MDS or any other tough ultra, we can easily get caught up in the facts and figures. The distance, the conditions, the terrain, the kit and ratio of people that drop out, but when the 'WHY' is big enough the facts really do not matter.

Are you kidding yourself?

A word of warning on this. You cannot just pick out a reason why that has no relevance to you and that doesn't match your values. The desert will find it out and prise you and your half-arsed 'reason why' apart. Just like the runner from 2016 I write about elsewhere in this book. He had re-mortgaged his house to take part in the race and had in the past completed over 100 Ironman events yet halfway up a jebel he turned and strolled back to the check point to pull himself out of the race. He looked in great shape, he was injury free and had all the kit, knowledge, experience and physical attributes he needed to complete the MDS… he just didn't have a big enough reason to be there.

Some people just know their reason why, others are not sure, but know they want to finish it, both can be strong enough to get you through, but maybe you want to heighten the desire a little more? Perhaps you haven't yet discovered your why? In any case I have created a short exercise that you can do as often as you feel necessary to truly find your reason why so that the facts of the MDS no longer matter to you.

Step 1 – Establish your highest values.

You can work through the steps listed below or download an easy to follow worksheet at runninglightbook.com/resources

In the table below, I have listed over 50 of the most common values. Read through the words and shortlist 8-10 that resonate with you most or that just feel or sound right. After that, work with your shortlisted values and arrange them into order of importance to you. Your highest value first and least high of the shortlist last.

Authenticity	Faith	Meaningful Work
Achievement	Fame	Openness
Adventure	Friendships	Optimism
Authority	Fun	Peace
Autonomy	Growth	Pleasure
Balance	Happiness	Popularity
Beauty	Honesty	Religion
Boldness	Humour	Reputation
Compassion	Influence	Respect
Challenge	Inner Harmony	Responsibility
Recognition	Justice	Security
Citizenship	Kindness	Self-Respect
Community	Success	Service
Competency	Status	Spirituality
Contribution	Knowledge	Stability
Creativity	Leadership	Trustworthiness
Curiosity	Learning	Wealth
Determination	Love	Wisdom
Fairness	Loyalty	

Step 2 - Keep the top 5 and discard the rest.

We have roughly established your top 5 values. These are the things that are important to you. Now brainstorm the reasons why you want to complete the MDS. Think about all the things you will gain and lose from being successful and how you can use them in the future. Also think about any other people that could benefit from your success? Remember that there is no right or wrong answer for this and if you have purely selfish reasons then that's fine. Nobody can judge because they don't understand your 'why', these are your values and your reasons and only you need to understand them.

Step 3 - Compare each reason to your values

Now take each reason one at a time and compare it to your values. How does it relate to each of your values and how does it help you meet and satisfy your values?

Example: Value = Adventure. Ask 'how does the MDS satisfy my highest value of adventure?' The answer here is obvious and I am sure you can list lots of ways it satisfies the value, but sometimes it isn't that easy and you need to work a little harder to establish the links.

It can be normal to have some values that are not satisfied by doing the MDS, but in that case, you should be able to link it to another of your values. If you can't, you have some work to do.

By now you should have identified some powerful reasons for going through the pain and hard work associated with the MDS or any other event you are planning. Each should obviously relate to your values because if they don't you are very unlikely to succeed. When your 'Why' aligns with and helps you fulfil your highest values we become unstoppable. This is where the super-human acts originate from and at this point the facts no longer matter. The desire to succeed is so strong inside that you will find a way to overcome obstacles, by-pass pitfalls and scale any hurdles in your way.

After identifying your why, you may have become aware of a trend within your answers. Do you know that people are motivated in different ways? Some people are motivated in a towards manner and others are motivated in an away from manner. A great example of this is weight loss. Some people are motivated because they no longer want to be fat, suffer from weight related illness and ailments or are fed up of living with guilt and shame. They are away from motivated. They are motivated by moving away from the pain. The other end of the spectrum is a towards pleasure motivation. Instead of being inspired by moving away from the pain they have a desire to look better, be thinner, wear more fitting and flattering clothes and want compliments from those around them about how good they look.

Recruit your mode of motivation

Scan over your values work and see if you can identify what mode motivates you and we can use that to not only build motivation but multiply it and turn it into determination. Remember that motivation gets you going and determination keeps you going.

If you are towards motivated, you will respond better by celebrating the wins and progress you make towards the event, but be careful that you do not start too far out. Naturally, we will be less motivated the further we are from our motivation origin.

Personally, I started my preparation way too far out and didn't really get going or start taking it seriously until I had been to the MDS Expo. If you are towards motivated then you would benefit from lots of little events and reminders of where you are going. Images of previous race medals, case studies from historic runners and a countdown on your phone screen as reminders would work for you.

On the flip side, those that are away motivated would benefit from tracking their weight loss or fitness progress by comparing them against where they started. Alternatively, reminders of times and events where you failed or did not finish would motivate you by agitating the feelings you felt at those times.

Bare your mode of motivation in mind as you consider the motivation agitators below.

Establish your motivation agitators

In this section, I want to present not only the importance of having motivation agitators but also offer you some suggestions as to how you can create your own powerful reminders of your big reason WHY.

Motivation agitators remind me of my childhood. I loved nature. My favourite past time was catching frogs and newts or collecting caterpillars and other bugs, but one day I learnt a very valuable lesson. Maybe it was boredom? Maybe it was curiosity? Maybe I was showing off... Perhaps it was just grade A, premiership level stupidity...? Whatever it was that led me to poke the fuck out of a wasp's nest that day I have no idea. I just know that I went from cocky little shit to squealing child in seconds. I had been aware of the wasp nest deep in the muddy grass bank below the flats where we lived for a good few weeks. I remember the wasps appearing one day and a little nervous at first I skipped frog collecting for a while and stayed away. After a few weeks or gradually creeping closer I became comfortable with the wasps. They never really bothered me as I lifted logs and stones under their flight path and soon enough I was happy to even check some of my favourite froggy hiding places within inches of the nest. I believe we could have lived in harmony if I had left the wasps to do what wasps do, but... as you can probably guess I decided against that.

I went on a one boy mission to rid Yorkshire of

wasps and started prodding, digging and clawing at the entrance to the nest. The wasps got a little faster and closer at first, but I didn't really pay much attention. That is until what seemed like a cloud of marauding insects attacked every orifice on my body. ... and I mean every orifice! I was violently stung all over my body. I think the most severe sting was in the white of my eyeball. My mum spent the remainder of the day bathing my little bumps with chamomile lotion but with zero sympathy.

So, the wasps are very much like your reason why. Left untouched it will bubble around and be present, but never really have any gravity to it. We become accustomed to it. It becomes benign unless we agitate it regularly. Every day and as often as required, we need to poke and prod our motivation with little reminders. Instead of letting it drift around us we need to slap ourselves across the face with it at every opportunity.

Keep your 'Why' in plain view.

Consider implementing as many of the motivation agitators listed below.

You can find many other ways to agitate your motivation in the Running Light Facebook group and I encourage you to share your own unique ways to help others.

Away Motivated

- Post-it's with pain orientated messages and reminders

- Post photos of failures, DNF's and before pictures etc. around the house, on your computer screen and next to your bed, fridge for example.

- Spend ten minutes every day sitting quietly thinking about your away motivation and the consequences of not progressing

- Commit to watching 10-15 mins of videos or scan through old pictures of yourself at a time and status that you do not want to experience again each week

- Ask your close family and friends to encourage you with away motivators and give them examples so they understand

- Identify key milestones in your improvement and design low cost and low effort ways to celebrate reaching each milestone

- Write an abbreviation of your goal in the condensation every time you shower

- Create a bedtime self-hypnosis script (Learn how at RunningLightBook.com/Resources)

- Write a letter to yourself as you have success- fully completed the MDS that lists all the things you are working towards. Read the letter each week or when you find yourself questioning why you are committing to this

Towards motivated

- Post-its with future orientated messages and reminders

- Countdown tick chart or phone / PC screen saver

- Spend ten minutes every day sitting quietly thinking about you're toward motivation and the consequences of not preparing correctly

- Commit to watching 10-15 mins of MDS videos on YouTube every week

- Use the 1-second everyday app to capture 1 second of your progress each day and commit to reviewing the film reel at the end of each week

- Ask your close family and friends to encourage you with towards motivators and give them examples so they understand

- Identify key milestones in your progress and design low cost and low effort ways to celebrate reaching each milestone

- Write an abbreviation of your goal in the condensation every time you shower

In addition, I would recommend hiring a coach or trainer. The minimum should be an accountability partner or group that you speak to each week. Research has shown that the fear of letting someone down is a powerful motivator when willpower is low.

In this chapter, we have explored your big reason why. Without a big reason, why we have these little things like 'facts' in the way but they don't have to. You may recognise all the different ways you are lacking in motivation... *but...* people change and you're a person, so you can change too. In the next few chapters we will look at beating fears.

CHAPTER 6

BIGGEST FEARS
AM I ENOUGH???

'If you think you are or you think you're not... you're right'

Henry Ford (Adapted)

The number 1 fears or challenges that all the people that completed the survey revolved around fitness, robustness and physical preparation. I have a section dedicated to fitness later in the book, but the solution to these fears are in the mindset and I thought it best placed here.

Story...

I understand why fitness is the most common fear because it's tangible. Each time we run we get immediate feedback that our heart and lungs are working. Our legs ache and we recognize each step as another meter or so towards preparing for the MDS. It's the same in weight loss and weight management too. Each week I meet up to 25 weight loss clients that believe the answer to their issues is in fitness. Although I work in the fitness industry, am an advanced personal trainer and have coached thousands to look better and be fitter, I'm not going to be outlining the training programmes that are 6 parts Mo Farah to 4 parts Roger Bannister.

This book isn't the same as others because I want to concentrate on the mind and recruit that as the hub of everything we achieve. We will explore how fitness, kit and food are the tyre on the bigger wheel, but the central hub is our mind! Get that turning and spinning at the right velocity and we multiply the other factors. Instead of chatting purely about what distances, speeds and cadence you should be running at, we will explore the 'why' when we know what to do, when... with all the experience and resources we need, we don't do what we know!

It's like trying to eat healthier. We all know that Krispy Kreme's or that third glass of wine isn't good for us, but we still consume it. Why...we don't DO what we know? Look on any high street around the country now. You will see so many people that know how to stay in shape and are working to stay in shape... but it looks like the shape they are chasing is a soddin' beach ball! They don't DO what they Know. It's the same as writing this book. I know that the key to finishing a book... a bit like finishing the MDS, is consistent effort. Small, continuous steps. One step at a time, one word at a time, but over a prolonged period. I know that... but that's not what I have done. Life gets in the way. For a period, I kept finding excuses for putting the writing off. 'Oh, I have more important things to do'. 'My laptop is dead...', 'I'll just have an extra hour in bed!' If we did what we know, things would be easy and we would get results.

The truth is our subconscious mind controls everything we do. Even if we feel we have used our conscious mind to decide, we very seldom have. Each thought we have must pass through the subconscious mind for us to act and the little 'fecker' gets in the way sometimes. No wait, scratch that... it gets in the way a lot!!!

As the image below shows, we think and conceive with our conscious mind and we believe that this then controls our actions and behaviour. That seems obvious, but how many times have you gone to do something intentionally and you do something completely different... even if you had made a conscious effort NOT to do the it in the first place?

Studies of the mind have shown us that thoughts and ideas pass through the subconscious mind before we act. Many things such as our beliefs, experiences, values, ethics and our self-identity or self-image get in the way and often sabotage our actions. We will explore some in this book and I'll give you a few strategies to beat it, but now I want to illustrate it with a story.

Before I met my beautiful wife Paula, I never

seemed to have much 'luck' with women. I always seemed to end up with grade A crack pots with the compassion of Hannibal Lecter. Similar to ladies that cannot help themselves with the bad boys, I always ended up making poor choices with partners. I was poisoned, stabbed and one particular pyscho-bitch from hell tried to gouge my eye out with a key. So how was I so unlucky that I always ended up with these idiots? Well the truth is it was my own doing. During counselling for symptoms of PTSD I discovered that my self-esteem and confidence was so low it affected how I acted. Fearing rejection, I never really chased the women that I liked. I froze when I met nice women and always ended up with women that came on to me and they were always the nutters. Each time I broke up I would swear 'never to get into a relationship with a woman like that again'. Consciously I would commit to finding a woman with traits that were completely opposite of those the poisoners and eye gougers had. The problem was my sub-conscious hadn't changed and not long after making that promise to myself I would find myself having the same, 'you could do so much better' conversation with my mum again, lol.

In this chapter, we have explored that rationally, we believe fitness will hinder us during the MDS. We discovered that it runs deeper than that and it's our subconscious mind that will affect us most. You may recognise all the different ways you are sabotaging your progress, failing to train and beating yourself up but we can start to change that here. In the next few chapters we will look at changing the strategies deep with the subconscious mind. Right now, you may not except the theory that we can change it all just with the self-talk in our heads *yet* and that's fine. Everything is a process so promise me one thing? You will at least see the next chapter through to the end?

CHAPTER 7

I AM WORRIED I'M NOT FIT ENOUGH… **WHAT DOES FIT ENOUGH LOOK LIKE TO YOU?**

'Everyone has an in-built ability to survive & keep moving – When required!'

Dr Mike Stroud

Can you remember the first time you felt alone in the dark?

I think I was around 5 years old. I shared a bedroom with my older brother Joe… well his name is Carl… but we all called him Joe. I know it's weird right, but anyway back to the story. Joe and I, like all siblings, tormented each other relentlessly. We were the best of buddies and incredibly close, but at times we didn't see eye to eye. We had a tit for tat battle throughout our childhood, I would scratch his Top Gun soundtrack LP and he would burn my Star Wars figures in the fire. He jumped on me from the top bunk so I filled his wellies with frog spawn. Anyway... for some reason Joe went away for the night. I was looking forward to having a torment free bedroom for the night, but something strange happened as Mum wished me good night and turned off the lights. I felt a strange feeling in my chest and stomach as soon as the light went off. My heart started pumping heavy and fast and all my senses were heightened. I couldn't settle and I sat bolt upright and with the pitch, volume and tone of a thousand banshees, screamed!

Mum came dashing in wondering what the hell had caused me to shriek so loudly. As she turned the light on I let out an audible sigh of relief, I smiled slightly and may have even let out a bit of wee, but that's not important. What's important is that nothing had changed in the room other than I could now see. Horrible beasties and monsters didn't suddenly scarper for the wardrobe or scramble under the bed, I could just see again. Fear comes from the not knowing, it feeds on time and can be crippling. To combat your biggest fears right now we need to shed light on 'it' to dispel the fear. We need to build a history of success and an unshakeable confidence in your abilities. All fears stem from the unknown.

Fear Everything And Run

Or

Face Everything And Rise?

When I got the results from my survey, the most common fears were obvious to see.

1. Am I fit enough?
2. Am I tough enough?
3. Am I prepared enough?

Actually, all three are the same fear. The fear of failure, but all dressed up in a slightly different manner. Think about the statements and what we now know about fear. The word enough? What the hell does that mean? My first question for you is what is 'enough' to you? I don't know what 'enough' is? Can I get a cup of enough please?

Do you?

Not knowing equals fear so let's get more specific and bring a little more clarity to this.

Now if 'enough' to you is finishing in the top 3, then I don't know, but if you were running at that level you probably wouldn't be reading this book or you are just reading it out of interest. If so, skip on.

If you mean 'enough' just to complete the MDS then I would ask:

What have you decided?

It really is a decision. Have you decided you are or are not? No seriously, it really is that simple. If you decide you are sufficiently fit, robust and prepared then you are. If not, then work to do. You're not on the start line yet so you still have time to make sure you are ready... but that doesn't mean training your legs!

If you think you are not enough, then I want you to do one thing. Think about the language and the words you are saying to yourself. In my experience, it will be something like 'I'm not fit enough', 'I am not robust enough' or 'I am not prepared enough' and I just want you to add the word 'yet' to the end of the statement. You may not believe this *yet* (See what I did?) but stick with it. The statements above are static statements. They do not suggest movement or progress from that point. Though your brain is inherently lazy, it is yours to use. It's a tool and like any tool it is subject to user error. Your language tells your brain to stop looking for ways to change the 'fact' you have stated. Adding the word 'yet' changes the statement. It now suggests movement and change and your brain no longer switches off. 'Yet' creates a bit of curiosity about the future. We get a touch more confident and may even get a little excited because of it. It works with any limiting decision that you have made.

'I'm not a millionaire' – No point trying to be then! Or 'I am not a millionaire yet!'

'I'm not a desert runner' – Feck' why am I

training for the MDS then? Or 'I am not a desert runner yet!' Pass me the mother chunking Bounce Ball and tape up my nipples... I'm going running and I won't be back for a fortnight!

It's a simple technique and one you may not be implementing yet... but you could start now. Your brain is your tool. Use it!

I believe in you

So back to the fears. I wrote previously about how I believe every able man and woman (and many disabled for that matter) on the planet has the potential to complete the race and I stand by that. At the end of each Running Light presentation I give, I plant a seed that everyone in the audience has the potential to complete the MDS. I get a lot of 'never', 'no way', 'why would I want to?' type replies, and I get some 'really... you believe that?' replies, but I believe in them regardless even if they refuse to and I believe in YOU. I believe it because cats climb, dogs hunt in packs, fish swim, sloths... wait what the fuck do sloths do? Anyway, birds fly and humans run! You were born for this. In the words of the great philosopher and songwriter Bruce Springsteen – 'Baby you were born to run!'

I was shocked at fitness being the number 1 fear or challenge. I couldn't believe just how many participants were petrified that they will not be fit enough. Maybe you are similar? They heaped the pressure on themselves and I know from my Royal Marines training days that that level of self-imposed pressure is stifling. It can stop you in your tracks and halt progress faster than anything. When coaching we call it paralysis by analysis and I'm sure you have experienced similar either in the past or right now.

The lion tamer

To illustrate this, I want you to think of a circus lion tamer. Picture the scene, the barrel-chested fella stands in the centre of the ring with a huge cat roaring in front of him. He controls the big cat, huge teeth and gigantic claws with the rapid crack of the whip… but does he?

It's easy to think the whip does all the work because its loud and moves fast, but it's the chair that keeps the lion at bay. Without the chair, the lion would lunge forward and chew the lion tamers face off, but the chair stops it in its tracks. The reason is because the chair has 4 legs. With just one the lion would knock the leg out of the way. The four legs cause the lion to be reactive. It doesn't know which leg will come at him first so the lion must sit back and wait. It's the same with your training right now. Life is potentially throwing more than one thing at you right now or you're piling the pressure on yourself by analysis.

The Facebook group seems to be the biggest cause of paralysis by analysis as people share what they are and are not doing. The key is to remember that as with all events, each participants' needs will be very different. It can depend on so many things from previous training experience to your race goals. Someone competing for a top 100 finish will need to train much differently from those of us with our hearts set on just completing it. It's ok for your training to be different from others, it's fine if you are not doing the miles that others are or haven't laced your trainers for the 20th time yet.

I was amazed at some of the answers and knew that a large proportion of MDS runners who compare themselves to elite runners and other people they know nothing about. So many were living in the 'gap'! Not Watford Gap… though if there seemed to be a nucleus of ultra-running nuts centralized around a specific geographical area it would be worth investigating, it's a different gap. Before we get into that, consider this. One participant remarked that they are walking between 60 and 100 miles each week, were doing it with a little kit and this was around 9 months from the start of the event. Great preparation, I thought, but as I examined the results further I was shocked. This person's biggest fear was not being fit enough AND his aim was simply to complete the MDS! I wanted to shake him and scream "do you not realise just how far ahead of the curve you are???' The truth was, he didn't. He couldn't see it. He was proof that often when we are in the frame we cannot see the picture. At that time, I was running a couple of times a week (if that) and I knew one lady that, despite being just 5 months from the MDS, had not even run more than 10k in her life!

Every MDS runner needs to take a huge mouthful of rationality juice here. Imagine having the best MDS you can possibly have. That's what I want you to have. I want you to enjoy every minute of the preparation and event itself and that does not mean you torture yourself with irrational thoughts about should's, could's, must's, would of's and wish I'd's...

Horizon thinking.

Time and time again experience shows that most of the thousands I work with, suffering from similar irrational and damaging thoughts live in what we call the 'gap'. The gap is a horrible place to live because nothing is ever good enough, days are miserable and your ability to recognise positive is diminished. The gap is keeping up with the jones's or, in this case, keeping up with the elite runners! It comes from all those times when your teachers made out you weren't good enough and the truth is... us humans came a little pre-wired to fall into this way of thinking.

Seriously! Scouring the landscape kept us alive as cavemen and cave women. We are pretty mediocre animal. We don't have any sharp teeth or claws, we have no armour or camouflage, we're not particularly fast or strong and even our genitals are on the outside of our body so we were vulnerable back in the day. We had every reason to be wary of anything that rustled in the undergrowth or any unnatural disturbance of long grass or vegetation that caught our eye.

Early in our development as kids we discovered a line within the landscape that captured our imagination. It's always there and we call it the horizon. It's the point when the land meets the sky. The problem begins when we try to get to it. When we set our goals on reaching that point and we start walking towards it. The horizon just keeps moving. We cannot reach it because though we can see the point in our vision, in reality it doesn't really exist.

Sometimes, because of the lay of the land we appear to get quite close, then as we summit a hill we see the horizon has leapt to the next hill or is at the end of a sprawling expanse.

Imagine that following a successful MDS, you set a new challenge. A challenge to reach the horizon and you set off and each day you walked and walked for miles through rolling valleys and across long stretching flatlands. Each day you stop to measure your progress and the damn horizon is still just as far away from where you started? At that point, you are going to start questioning yourself. You may even start to get frustrated and a little angry. Perhaps you'll blame yourself and there is a great chance that you'll throw your towel in and give up? It isn't very motivating.

Though there is nothing wrong with setting our goals way out in the distance and aiming for the horizon, it's how we measure our progress that makes the difference. Measuring how far we have left to go is the problem. It extinguishes desire and defuses motivation. That's because aiming for the horizon is aiming for the ideal, the perfect outcome or solution. The sad truth is that the ideal doesn't exist. Occasionally we reach what we previously set as the ideal, but it rarely lasts long. Ever been ecstatic to get the latest phone or a new car only to want the next model not long after? This is called the arrival fallacy and I believe we have all suffered from this one at some point. You can spot it with phrases and thoughts listed below:

"It'll be fine when I'm earning £100,000 a year..."

"I'll be happy when I can buy a Ferrari..."

or... a little more relevant to us...

"If I can train every day I'll be ready for the MDS..."

"I should be running 20 miles a day by now..."

So, what is the answer? How do we stop ourselves from falling into this trap?

It's quite easy. Like I said before, it's perfectly fine to set our goals way out in the distance, but the key to creating unshakable motivation, building unwavering consistency, being truly happy with your progress, lifting the dark heavy blanket of self-doubt and self-imposed pressure is to measure your progress on how far you have come.

Have lofty goals. Chase the horizon, but use your footprints to see how well you are doing. In my experience, more people have changed their lives and their lifestyles, by making this shift than any other factor. Ditching horizon thinking and measuring against the 'ideal', in exchange for recognising the progress they have made instead.

This shift doesn't always come easy, but with consistent effort, it can become fixed in your life for good.

3 biggest wins

To train your brain to look for progress as opposed to perfection, I encourage my clients to do a little exercise each night. Every night I ask them to write down 3 significant moments of progress that they have experienced that day. Three small wins that along with the progress recognised from the last few days, start a motivational snowball rolling. A snowball that will continue to grow and gather speed until it is truly unstoppable.

I then ask them to plan three further wins for the next day. Our mind will look for whatever we tell it to. We can predispose our brain to look for whatever we tell it to and this quick and easy exercise recruits a powerful technique that all the elite level athletes know. More on that later, just be happy with how far you have come to date. If you are not happy with your progress right now you have a decision to make. Have you failed to make the progress you want because life got in the way? Maybe, like me, you've had a stinker of a year? If, being 100% honest with yourself, you've tried your best and it is what it is? If that's the case, then it does not mean you are doomed. On the other hand, if you have had every opportunity to train and prepare and you have failed yourself it's time to make a commitment and start making small steps towards a more motivated and more disciplined you.

The problem with a training program

If you are preparing for the MDS, you will have a training program in place? You can see my initial one on the MarathonDesShambles.com blog where I set out each phase of my preparation. It would be interesting watching for anyone, but there is a problem with plans.

I'll call back on my military experience again here as I did more planning in those days than you can imagine. Ever heard the saying 'military precision'? Maybe you are thinking that military operations run without a hitch with each individual soldier knowing exactly what he is to do and at what time. Sorry to burst your bubble but that never works out. In fact, it never works that way.

In the military, there is a saying, 'no plan survives contact with the enemy'... Actually, there are two sayings... 'the first casualty of war is the plan.' I'm serious, nothing in the military goes to plan because there are events you cannot account for or that you cannot predict. A little like your life. Little did I know the lease on my business would be pulled from under me midway through my MDS preparation. As I wrote out my program I could never have predicted my wife getting ill, losing half my staff within the space of a week, our family dog of 14 years dying, my brother having an operation on his back, my dad severing nerves in his hand in an industrial accident, my mother retiring, my long-lost son (who I hadn't heard from in 14 years) suddenly getting in touch and eventually coming to live with Paula and I... It's all life and actually... I was praying for the MDS as a break from it all lol.

So, what do the military do? Knowing the plan will go out of the window the minute that they cross the start line, the military relies on individual skills and knowledge of standard procedures to get them through. Through months of rehearsals and practice, each component knows how to operate if things go wrong. The sum of the whole subsequently becomes exponentially more effective than the individual parts.

So what? Well, I encourage people to look at component factors in their fitness when they are creating the plan. A traditional marathon training program consists only of running. The only variety is how much of running you do each day and at what intensity. But here's the problem and I will need a signal to know I am on the right track... a nod of the head, a small smile, even an audible 'yep' but definitely not some crazy American 'HELL YEAH!'...

Running programs involve lots of running. i.e. 'HOURS' of running, like endless, mind-numbing trots along long country roads or tow paths. Couple that with another fact. MDS training, overall, takes place in the cold, dark winter months of the UK. You are, to coin a phrase, on to a shitter!

Hours of long boring runs in the cold, wet,

wintry months is not really what I signed up for. In fact, on some mornings during February before the MDS, I was praying the old dog would die so I had an excuse not to go!

So, here's the equation. We have our plan, a running plan because we are doing a running event. We try to shoehorn hours of long, boring runs into a crazy busy lifestyle that is unpredictable and all during a time when the weather in the UK is at its worst. The evenings and mornings are pitch black and THEN we beat ourselves up when things don't go so well. I mean we 100% abuse ourselves! Crikey if we spoke to others the way we speak to ourselves we'd get punched in the face!

Did you know you are a running machine? No serious, you have evolved to run. If we buy a Ferrari and put it a showroom for 30 years, does it stop being a fine Italian sports car? No... some of the components may get a little rusty or stiff (...sound like your lower back perhaps?) and it's the same for you. Deep down your body is built for running. You're not a super-fast powerhouse like a Ferrari that's for sure. Humans are more like a Mondeo. We just need to get you road worthy again. You could start by ditching a little of the excess baggage in the boot (lose a few pounds), loosening the joints and suspension a little (increase your flexibility) clear out the old contaminated fuel and replace with cleaner fuel. I think you get my point here?

On the accompanying website to this book, you will find a handy assessment tool to help you with your component parts. You can find it at RunningLightBook.com/Resources

The human body is an amazing chassis for an event such as this you just need to update some of the component parts. I ditched many of the loooooong boring runs in the naff weather for yoga and stretching sessions to increase flexibility and work out the tight (injury susceptible) areas in my body, ditched sugar and alcohol from Christmas onwards and scorched 10 kg in excess weight easily, worked on leg and core strength and ensured I was as heat ready as I could be with the resources I had available. Great news... I'm still alive and I made it!

It is so easy to get caught up in what everyone else is doing when you see people's updates on Facebook, it can stifle your preparation and even stop you completely in your tracks if you let it. It is easy to get caught up in the addictive nature of such an active Facebook group. There is also a lot of drama in there too.

The Drama Triangle

The Drama Triangle is a model of dysfunctional social interaction, created by psychotherapist Stephen Karpman. Like the fire triangle, each point of the triangle represents a player within a drama.

There are 3 roles within any drama.

1. The victim – Most often in the Face group it is the person posting.

2. The persecutor – Family, job, kit, weight, partners, running partners, the weather... sometimes even the victim themselves!

3. Finally, there is the rescuer... aka you! Well certainly anyone that gets caught up in the post trying to solve the victim's problem or help them break free of the issues they face.

The problem with dramas is that they, like the fire triangle, become self-perpetuating if those three positions are filled. Let's take a late night boozy tiff between a couple as an example. I rarely drink now, but like I mentioned before I loved a good booze! I remember heading out with an old friend of mine and his girlfriend. I was home on leave from the Royal Marines and was in full on, 'super twat, single handed rid the world of Guinness' mode. The night was great despite my friend and his girlfriend having a wretched, pissed up gooseberry along. That is until it came time for us to make the decision every late-night reveller faces. Do we head home having had a great night or stay out and get turbo-pissed! The decision was an easy one for me. I was heading to a club and that was it and my friend's girlfriend had made her mind up too. She wanted to head home. So, it was Dan, my friend that was torn between us. He was keen on Sally; in fact, they are still together 20 years on they are still happily married with 2 great kids.

I think he wanted to head to a club with me. I had been away in Kosovo for a few months and we had some catching up to do, but he also wanted to head home with Sally. In the end, he did what every, irrational early twenties guy with far too many Bacardi Breezers under his belt would do. He created a drama! Looking back this is pretty cringe worthy and could have easily been avoided with compromise. I could have said, 'Don't worry Dan. You head home now and we will catch up tomorrow', maybe Sally could have said "right, we have had a great night and I'm ready to go home, but you stay out with Craig and I'll see you when you get home' Whatever... but that's not what happened.

Dan started a row with Sally. So, stop there. Right now, we have Dan the Persecutor and Sally as the Victim. To close the triangle, we just need a Rescuer. Who better than a chubby soldier that could barely stand up straight and was simultaneously trying to piss behind a skip and take a bite out of his kebab?

I'll save you the hassle of the dialogue, but just know that we then spiralled through the drama triangle for what seemed like and age. With Sally as the victim, Dan persecutor and me rescuer. Which spiralled to me as the persecutor and Dan the victim cos he was disrespecting his girlfriend and obviously Sally then started on me as the rescuer for giving Dan shit. Now I was the victim, Sally the persecutor and Dan then had to rescue me. It went on for ages. I am sure you have experienced situations like this with your own family r ' friends?

Mini dramas happen pretty much r

mins on the Facebook group. The unsuspecting get so caught up in it and sometimes even side dramas spin off from the main drama.

The shitty thing with Sally, Dan and I was that by the time we had sorted it out (and we were all going to get wankered with Craig in the club!) The club had stopped letting people in and we couldn't get a taxi! We then had a full-on drama packed walk all the way home.

The arguments were futile, but we get so caught up in them. I understand that people want to help people and that there are people on the group that genuinely need help, but be aware of the drama triangle. Are you getting caught up in a drama that is stealing your time, energy and resources and preventing you from doing what you need to be doing?

Surviving Facebook

Personally, I heavily restrict the time and energy I give to Facebook. It can be tough, but here are a couple of things that you can do to help:

1. Set time limits: Pre-set the amount of time that you will give to FB and stick rigidly to that schedule.

2. Use your password as a reminder: I would ensure that I was logged out every time I visited FB and then set my password to an MDS related reminder.

'IsThisHelpingYourTraining4TheMDS'   or 'MarathonDesS8bles'

3. There's an app for that: I have an app on my phone called Cold Turkey. There are similar apps out there, but this app kills everything on your phone for up to an hour. The only thing you can do is make an emergency call. It's like true cold turkey for some phone and social media addicts. I use it when I arrive at the gym or need to focus and get some writing done.

Avoiding Drama

The best way to avoid drama is to understand the role you are being asked, forced or are on the brink of fulfilling. At that point, you must refuse to play your part. Stay out of it and focus on your own circle of influence (see the interview with performance coach Phil Quirk later in the book). If it is a genuine friend in need or you have vital input for someone struggling, you can message them privately to avoid drawing others in.

To end this section, I just want to say that the Facebook group is an immense resource full of huge pearls of wisdom, but just like the Force... it is open to abuse and can be used for good, or bad. You decide!

Forget What Others Are doing or Not Doing

Back to my original point of compr yourself to others and getting caught up '

own personal little drama. I recommend you focus on the constituent parts of your training. Head over to RunningLightBook.com/resources to take a short assessment. Have confidence in what your body has been designed to do AND any runs are a bonus. You will find that taking the strain off yourself like this will change your mindset about your runs. You will want to go because you want to go, not because you feel you should... oh and you may well enjoy it a lot more. What we resist often persists.

Training in The Hole

In addition to living in the hole, the large proportion of society 'train in the gap'. At TEAM Bootcamp, we deliver a smart training programme that has two extremes. The first is lung busting, heart splitting, muscle smashing, high intensity training and the second is long, slow volume type training. Science has proven that both training protocols have widely different effects on the human body and fitness in general. We instil in our clients not to aim for the highest peaks as the marker of how effective their training is, but to measure the gulf between their most intense and lowest intensity sessions. Very little adaptation comes from training the mean levels of intensity other than connective tissue become strained and we expose our joints, muscles and connective tissues to overuse issues.

We call these training areas 'the hole' at TEAM which is a lot like homeostasis in regular exercises.

You will experience massive gains in your training and physical abilities by aiming to widen the gap between long, slow, low intensity training sessions such as hill walking, long runs (10k plus, 20k plus for more experienced runners) and high intensity sessions where you feel like you have just shit out a lung. An intensity that you cannot sustain for more than a few minutes, 20 mins max. If you finish flat packed on the floor a with a face as red as Hell Boy you're in the right zone.

Other benefits

Other benefits of training at the two intensity extremes are huge. Though the long, slow, steady sessions consume more time, they can be a great escape from busy life and are excellent for testing your kit and clothing for the MDS. They give you time to think and work on the other psychological techniques on this book such as agitating your big 'why' and running your 'If, Then' strategies which I outline later in the book. Physiologically you are increasing the amount of energy stores in your muscles and improving your body's ability to take in and use oxygen. Time spent moving at this intensity is great for preparing your mind for the long days in the desert during the MDS and give you an opportunity to uncover the component that will dictate whether you get a finishers medal more than anything else… your self-talk!

The high-intensity sessions have other benefits such as increasing strength, power and spe Each are often neglected by distance ru' but all are important for powering up dunes and through sand. High-intensity training will increase your body's ability to dissipate waste products such as carbon dioxide and lactic acid. Recently we needed to convert a couple of rooms at our residential camp as we had reached a sticking point. The unaware thought Paula and I were daft because we converted two perfectly good bedrooms into bathrooms.

Everyone else focused on increasing bed spaces and therefore potential revenue, but Paula's experience told her that without the ability to get rid of waste and maintain cleanliness the entire camp would halt. If we continue with this analogy, we can reinforce this lesson further. During planning the plumber explained that the key to getting a bathroom that works and functions is to get the waste pipes right! Getting water, furniture and the other resources needed in is the easy bit, but get the waste wrong and everything grinds to a halt.

It's the same with your body in the desert, you could force oxygen into your body and even intravenous sugar into your blood, but neither will make a difference if you cannot get rid of the waste. Waste during exercise comes in the form of by-products from exercise, namely lactic acid, carbon dioxide and heat!

Example high-intensity training sessions

I have provided some example high-intensity training sessions which you can use as they are or as examples to create your own workouts. Access them at http://runninglightbook.com/resources. I used each of the sessions in my last 6-week preparation for the MDS in 2016.

In this chapter, we have explored how you measure your progress and what your frame of reference is. Measuring on the 'ideal' is paralysing and puts us in the gap, but there is another frame of reference to measure ourselves against. You may recognise all the different ways you are living in the gap... *but*... people change and you're a person, so you can change too. In the next few chapters we will look at your expectations and how we can take them and turn them into powerful road maps for overcoming pitfalls, hurdles and barriers.

CHAPTER 8

WHAT DO YOU
EXPECT?

A young woman went to her mother and told her about her life and how things were so hard for her. She did not know how she was going to make it and wanted to give up. She was tired of fighting and struggling. It seemed as one problem was solved a new one arose.

Her mother took her to the kitchen. She filled three pots with water. In the first, she placed carrots, in the second she placed eggs, and the last she placed ground coffee beans.

She let them sit and boil without saying a word. In about twenty minute she turned off the burners. She fished the carrots out and placed them in a bowl. She pulled the eggs out and placed them in a bowl. Then she ladled the coffee into a bowl. Turning to her daughter, she asked, "Tell me what you see?"

"Carrots, eggs, and coffee," she replied.

She brought her closer and asked her to feel the carrots. She did and noted that they were soft. She then asked her to take an egg and break it. After pulling off the shell, she observed the hard-boiled egg. Finally, she asked her to sip the coffee. The daughter smiled, as she tasted its rich aroma.

The daughter then asked, "What's the point, mother?"

Her mother explained that each of these objects had faced the same adversity... boiling water – but each reacted differently. The carrot went in strong, hard, and unrelenting. However, after being subjected to the boiling water, it softened and became weak. The egg had been fragile. Its thin outer shell had protected its liquid interior. But, after being through the boiling water, its inside became hardened. The ground coffee beans were unique, however. After they were in the boiling water they had changed the water.

"Which are you?" she asked the daughter. "When adversity knocks on your door, how do you respond? Are you a carrot, an egg, or a coffee bean?"

What do you expect?

The question above isn't a patronising challenge nor is it a rhetorical question. It's a serious question. I wonder what people expect when the sign up for the MDS. Obviously, you will expect many of the common things that the race is famed for such as the 50-degree heat, sandy terrain, sand storms, long distances and blisters to name a few. You must expect these not as 'in the way', but obstacles 'along the way'. The aim of this book is to get you to think differently and think at a deeper level. Having those expectations give us one-half of a powerful good habit forming, bad habit beating psychological strategy that will help you know you are on the right track, maintain your motivation and alleviate stress and self-imposed pressure.

If-then statements are a great way to pre-frame your actions in specific events, times and places. It takes the thinking out of decision making when you are fatigued, dehydrated, emotional and generally struggling, but can also reassure you and help you maximise the good times during positive moments.

Step 1 – We start with an 'If'. Actually, a list of 'If's'. You can either download the worksheet at RunningLightBook.com/Resources or use a simple piece of paper and list as many expectations as you can for the race. Here are a few examples.

- If I am nervous on the start line
- If I am suffering from heat illness

- If I struggle with the sand dunes
- If I run out of water
- If I think I am lost
- If I need the toilet along the route
- If I am much slower than I planned
- If I am much faster than I planned

The list can be huge, but I would set a strict time limit of 10 minutes to list your If's before moving on to your 'Then' statements.

Step 2 – We complete each If sentence with the word 'then' and a positive strategy to follow when faced with the event.

Examples:

If I am nervous on the start line, **then** I will remember that it is perfectly normal. Allow my body to breath freely, take in the sights and sounds, chat to the people around me and remember why I am here.

If I am suffering from heat illness **then** I will stop immediately before severe symptoms kick in. Find shade or ensuring my head is covered. Slowly sip water along with extra salt tablets and give myself enough time to recover before continuing. Think about the bull story which I will tell you later in the book!

By playing the **if-then** statements in your head you are creating new memories and eventually new neuro pathways. Essentially you have thought about most of the potential issues you could face before you even get there. Having a strategy also gives you the faith you require for optimum performance. You will learn that in the next chapter.

But what if the unexpected happens? Well... let's play it through...

If the unexpected happens **then** I will stop, take stock, think about the real-time evidence being presented to me. Remember that we naturally give negatives more gravity and allow a little time for my rational part of the brain to kick in. Then I will adjust my race strategy as required.

The key is to keep your 'If's' quite broad so they encompass more and you require less if-then statements. If I come across challenging terrain' for example could be hilly, rocky, downhills or even sandy river beds. It is ok to have some more specific if-then statements for obvious events such as large sand dunes.

One that I remember was the If I come across a large sand dune.

I often think what that the 100 Ironman vet that threw in the towel on the large Jebel would have done if he had had the same if-then statement for large hills as I did?

If I come across a large sand dune **then** I will drink and snack about 10 minutes away then cruise up at my own pace, minimise time at the top and pick up time on the downhill. Only after taking in the sights for a few seconds at the summit.'

I learned in the military to drink water and

snack before climbing the hill. It seems obvious to me that you need burst of energy from sugary snacks for the climb not at the top when the work is done and I also want the extra water required to already be in the stomach being absorbed by the time I get to the top. Many others marched straight up the hill only to collapse at the top gasping for water and energy while a little chubby Yorkshire man strolled past.

I employed a similar If-Then at checkpoints. **If** I spot a checkpoint **then** I will drink the contents of my bottles and eat part of my snack. My aim, in a tortoise and the hare way, was to minimise time in the checkpoint, maintain a consistent pace and avoid stiffening up by standing around too much.

Same for the finish line each day. **If** I see the finish line **then** I will start my recovery then. I'll make up my recovery shake and eat any remaining snacks in my pouches.

How much comfort can you take from knowing exactly how you will react to the challenges you have ahead? You should also use and practice your If-Then statements during training runs and other aspects of your life. Ditching a few of those excess pounds for example. **If** I need to grab lunch on the fly **then** I will opt for 100g of deli meat, two plums and a handful of nuts.

If I am invited out at Christmas, **then** I will explain I am in training will have a couple of drinks then switch to water to avoid over consumption and spoiling my training for the following day.

The 'then' aspect is completely up to you.

Whether you use mine or create your own they really are the best way to create faith in your training and throughout the race by being proactive.

In this chapter, we have explored your expectations and created tactics to help you make the best decisions we can with rational thinking, rather than burying our heads and having to deal with obstacles during the event in a much more irrational state. It may seem like a chore to create lots of if-then statements, but you can start with a 10-minute brainstorm to get started. After that, you can create them as you go along and experience issues in your training. All these work towards an unshakable internal dialogue which may seem hard to control right now, but you are already well on your way. In the next chapter, we will look at nurturing the perfect race day mindset for you.

CHAPTER 9

RACE DAY
MINDSET

'Whatever the mind can conceive the body can achieve'

Napoleon Hill

Before the race starts

Before the race starts you are going to have a few things going on mentally. Take a minute to picture what you will experience. Lots of people feel a lot of excitement and nervousness and take it as a negative anxious thing.

You can get a better picture by reading my race diary at the back of this book. Briefly, you have arrived in Morocco, had a long road journey with lots of other nationalities and people buzzing anticipating the event. Once in the desert and have another couple of days to sort kit, get medically checked and ensure everyone is ready to start the race. There is quite a lot of waiting around for the first couple of days and we know that fear feeds on time and you have lots of time to sit and dwell on things and really you just want to get going. A bit like ripping a plaster off. I recommend you just sit with the emotions for a while and let them be. No need to try and fight them. Take in the surroundings and the incredible uniqueness of the event. Just know that before long... and the time must countdown, you will be on the start line soon enough and before long you will be underway.

I recommend you make use of the time before the race as rest. You have done lots of travelling so make sure you spend the time resting, hydrating and fuelling ready for the race.

It is easy with the spare time available to start second guessing the choices you have made. Lots of runners are constantly arranging and rearranging their kit, food and clothing. If you complete the tips and techniques in this book then you will not fall victim to that. You will truly be happy with the decisions you have made and what more do you need really? Everything else is out of your control.

As you approach the start line, it really is an immense feeling. Music is playing, the banners are flying, helicopters are doing fly-by's buzzing the large lycra covered crowd forming around the start line. Patrick Bauer the race organiser, climbs on top of a Land Rover along with an interpreter to address the crowd. The air is electrified as 12-18 months of preparation culminates at this point.

What really stood out to me was the bright running clothing and the number of nations taking part. There were so many different types of bags, some with walking poles and some without, some with long sleeves and some with short. It seemed like no two people were dressed alike. In a group of 1300 runners in the same event and in the same conditions, I thought that was unbelievable and indicative that kit doesn't play much of a part, but how you feel about the kit does.

All the runners just want to get going and you should expect that you will feel nervous and you will also feel excited and that's perfect! What you have there are two of the three ingredients you need to help you perform at your best.

One is nervousness. It reminds us that what we are about to undertake has consequences to us personally. Consequences that are both negative if it goes wrong, but also positive when we get it right.

The second is excitement. Which feels very similar to nervousness. All we need now is the third ingredient, faith!

Faith in our abilities, faith in our kit and choices and faith in the people around us. Once again, after working through the exercises in this book and after consuming all the resources and content you will have faith in every aspect of your race. It's not for me to suggest that is already happening and you already feel much better about your race than you did before you picked up this book.

The formula for performing at your best is: Excitement + Nervousness x Faith = Optimal Performance.

Remember that optimal performance for you is the best you can do, with the time and resources you had available to prepare and with the natural ability you were born with.

The start of the race is marked by the rock song 'Highway to Hell' by AC/DC along with a loud hand held air horn. The crowd erupts and you slowly make your way over the start line. It takes a while for the back markers to pass the start line and as you do the pack starts to open up. Each day you will be faced with a group of excited runners jockeying for position. Getting buzzed by cameramen hanging out of the helicopters only adds to the occasion and it is very easy to go a little too hard and fast. I did it during the first leg of the 2016 race and I am sure many of you will too.

I got far too carried away at the start. The first leg was through what they called 'medium' sand dunes?! We had 12K of sand dunes couple with head on sand storms and I went too hard and fast. I was desperate to keep up with the front markers. My advice now is to hold back a little. You will catch many of those that start fast along the route, especially at the checkpoints where they must stop to cool, rearrange clothing and kit and hydrate or seek medical attention.

What I can also tell you is that what you see in the sand dunes is very much a mirage. I thought I was way back in the order of runners after a terrible first leg. I made it to the first checkpoint and headed straight for the medical tent with symptoms that were all too familiar to me. In the late 90's, I spent a large proportion of my Royal Marine years training in the tropical jungles of Brunei and Belize. I had experienced dehydration and heat exhaustion many times and have had to treat others with the same conditions. I stumbled into the medical tent looking for a little shade and shelter from the extreme heat which I was by no means physically prepared for. The medics started speaking about a drip in broken English and I really did not want the time penalty. I knew if I could consistently get small amounts of water on board, swallowed a few salt tablets and had a little food, I could get back on my feet. I hung around the medical tent for around 20 mins and the staff became more and more assertive. "If you are still here in 5 minutes, you are having a drip!"

I was starting to feel better and made my way back out into the hot desert sun just as my tent mate Peter entered the checkpoint. Pete was a great character despite being a GP with a wealth of experience. 'Bingo' I thought. Pete can check me out. I called over to him and before I even got the word 'dehydration' out of my mouth he challenged me. So, with the knowledge and experience gleaned from more than 20 years of practising medicine... he said, 'What are you doing in the spaz tent?'

'Pardon...?' I replied, taken back a little!

'Get out of the spaz tent and slow down a bit you numpty!'

Cheers Pete! Now I must say Pete was phenomenal regarding care and treatment and management of injuries in the tent group as well as those around us. He had also completely read the situation right and knew that the very fact I was walking out of the medical tent meant I was on the mend and could continue, but only after checking my ego at the door! I decided there and then IF I had to climb hills or came across soft sand THEN I would walk briskly instead of trying to run. This decision proved to be vital later in the event.

The second leg felt very long compared to the first and I was adamant, my stint in the 'spaz' tent had cost me dearly in the running order. I stopped for a short cool down and rehydration break another 3 times before the first day was complete. What seemed like hundreds of runners would pass me each time I stopped. The sheer number of footprints along the track suggested a thousand people had been there before me. I was shocked to find out later I had finished the first day in the top 25% of the race.

My point is, it is incredibly hard to gauge how well you are doing overall. Many of the fast starters will slow dramatically and lots of people in front will become injured or will spend a long time at checkpoints. Trying to guess how well you are doing during the leg is futile. Instead, focus on your strategies and look for the other signs and signals that you are doing well.

During each leg, you will be accompanied by your internal dialogue, which is now much more positive, supporting and kinder than others. Seriously, just look around and you will see people struggling with the mental battle taking place in their heads.

So how do we cope with some of the factors that will come into play psychologically? Factors such as the sheer distance you will cover, the weather and the terrain. The truth is you can do nothing about any of those three factors. To complete the race, you will have to cover the distance and terrain. That's part and parcel. During the race, I would constantly play a reminder in my head to ensure I only focussed on things I could influence and disregarded those I could not.

Many people who fail to read this book will

have records playing in their heads saying, 'I cannot do this!', 'this is too hard!', 'I'm struggling!', 'I'm going too slow!'... As I walked along I would say to myself 'It doesn't have to be fast, it doesn't have to be pretty... it just needs to be done!'

Another aspect that can create self-induced pressure is thinking about the sheer numbers who drop out each year. The dropout rate is another signal to the subconscious mind that this is risky. Whenever we hear of someone dropping out or being pulled out for medical reasons we don't really think about them. What we do is think about how we would react and feel if it was us that had failed. It places our subconscious on a heightened state of arousal each time we hear about another tent mate or co-runner dropping out.

As humans, we are hardwired to pick up on negatives and to give them more gravity than we give positives. It kept us alive as we roamed the earth 60,000 years ago. In fact, some research suggests that a negative thought can be up to 21 times more powerful than a positive thought. Let's put that into perspective for a minute. Imagine a negative thought equated to one mile. We would need 21 miles to offset that negative thought!

We survived by using our brains, communicating and by working together towards a common goal, but our evolutionary trait of focusing on negatives stays with us in our oldest and most primitive part of our mind.

Personally, I paid very little attention to drop out rates and it's not for me to suggest you do the same, but if you catch yourself dwelling on the number of dropouts bring your awareness back to the circle of things that you can influence, such as making sure your kit is ready for tomorrow, you are hydrated correctly, your feet are dressed and you have eaten as much as is comfortable. Also, think about the people that are still in the race. In 2016, it was reported that we lost more people on the first day than the total number from any other previous event. In fact, the race organisers added an extra hour to the cut-off time to ensure they didn't lose another 100 of the back markers and there were still more people in the race than out of it. The odds are still in your favour, remember that and remind others of the same.

I kept my personal self-talk simple along the way. I used the word 'but' a lot. But is a special word in our language. In our mind, it deletes anything that precedes it. The obvious example is 'I am sorry, but...' We don't pay attention to the 'I'm sorry' bit and focus on what comes next. 'I am sorry, but you were being a dick!'

Each time I caught myself thinking about the tough terrain I would end each internal statement with the word 'but'. I called it my 'but chaser!'

'Jeeze I hate sand dunes... but... at least it's not hard, sharp rocks!'

'I hate hard sharp rocks... but... at least it's not soft sand dunes!'

You get the picture. I even recall saying 'Well Pete's a good doctor... but he has the bedside manner of Beverley Allitt'

Practice using but chasers in your training runs and other training sessions and even in everyday life when you must deal with unpleasant or difficult circumstances. Practice, after all, makes permanent.

I would also spend a great deal of time thinking of two analogies. Maybe you could come up with similar stories to help you or, though it's not for me to suggest you should use these if you catch yourself in situations where you could easily work too hard and fight against the desert instead of working with it.

As I grew up I would spend most of my Sundays working the farm with my Grandad. In the morning, I would clean out the chickens and rabbits, pigs and horses and in the afternoon, we would muck out the cows or round up the sheep. I loved my time on the farm and learnt so much from my no-nonsense Grandad.

Once while standing in the field with my Grandad I asked him what time it was. To my amazement, he bent down and placing the flat of his hand under the udder of a milk laden cow he motioned to weigh the udder.

'Quart' to two' he said in broad Yorkshire

I have blown away and was speechless... 'Grandad... did I really just see that? Can you really tell the time by feeling the cow's udder?'

'Look. I'll teach you' he said. 'If you bend down and place your hand here...'

'Yes Grandad...' I said brimming with admiration from my Grandads wisdom.

'and you lift the udder ever so slightly...'

'Yes Grandad... got it... is it the weight of the milk...?'

'You can see the town hall clock in the village!'

But that's not the story I want to tell. My Grandad once told me of two bulls in the field. 'A lot like you and I' he said. 'One, a wise old bull that had lived well and had many happy years living in the pasture and one boisterous young bull. One day the young bull said "Grandad... look at those beautiful cows up in the next field. Let's run up there and shag one of them!"

'No, no' said the wise old bull. 'Let's walk up and shag them all!!!'

The bull story served as a reminder that the key to reaping the rewards was in slow steady consistent progress. Not rushing or working against the desert.

Another internal statement I keyed into my consciousness was to 'stick with the bow wave'. Have you ever waded a Land Rover before? I learned cross country driving skills in the Marines which included wading across rivers and ponds without stalling the vehicle. The key to navigating the river when the vehicle is almost completely submerged is to stay with the bow wave created by the forward motion of the vehicle. Too fast and the bow wave would fill the engine compartment and drown the engine. Too slow and the bow wave would catch up with the exhaust and engine and have the same effect.

The mental prompt to 'stay with the bow wave' reminded me that too fast and I didn't have the fitness, conditioning and hydration to cope and too slow and I would be out in the desert much longer, run the risk of running out of water and food, limit my rest and recover and mean more time spent on my already bloody, blistered plates of meat!

You may wonder why the stories? Well as I mention elsewhere in this book, stories are a great way to bypass the filter between your conscious and subconscious mind. Knowing, of course, that we act through our subconscious mind.

What happens if I just said don't go too slow or too fast?

Later in this book, I present how the mind has an inability to process a negative connotation.

- Wet paint – *Don't* touch! What happens?

- *Don't* think of a purple elephant! You did, didn't you?

It deletes the negative aspects of any statement. So, if you were to say to yourself 'Don't go too fast' and we delete the negative aspect what are we telling ourselves?

That's right. 'Go too fast'. That statement will also start a downward negative spiral of 'checks' by your subconscious looking to prove the statement right.

This is one of the reasons so many people fail to 'stop smoking' or 'stop eating fast food'.

Incredibly, the brain can scan the information presented to it by your 5 senses up to 5 times per second. It starts a spiral asking 'Am I eating fast food? Am I eating fast food? Am I eating fast food? Am I eating fast food? Shit... yes I have a big mac in my hand!'

If we relate it to the desert, we can do some psychological damage by thinking 'Don't go too fast' which our mind processes as 'go too fast' and our subconscious spirals with 'Go too fast? Go too fast? Go too fast?'

Imagine of we flipped the statement to a positive connotation and said, 'cruise at a steady pace', 'stay with the bow wave' or 'maintain the best pace for me'. It would start a positive spiral upwards or 'Am I still maintaining the best pace for me? Am I still maintaining the best pace for me?' The spiral continues.

After each day

I would use similar internal dialogue after each day. I would write me diary starting with all the tough and challenging aspects of the day. The tough legs, hilly terrain, sand storms and moments where I felt low or affected by the elements. I would write about missing home and how I thought about my friends and the people I had met in pain or that were out of the race and then write a huge BUT across the page. I would then write all the positives. I would look for the positive in every single moment. From the hundreds of different types and colours of sand, from the wildlife I saw, the locals I met and (being towards motivated **wink**) how much closer I was now I had completed the day.

By doing so I had released all the negatives and the lows from the day while capturing them in my diary, then deleted them with the but chaser so I could focus on the highlights. Of which there are so, so many!

In this chapter, we have explored some race day mind set techniques. You may recognise all the different ways you are beating yourself up mentally or creating anxiety about the MDS *but...* with a couple of minor changes to yourself talk you can change that. Start small and remember that practice makes permanent. We never completely get rid of negative talk so don't get overly concerned when shit thoughts creep back in. The key is to replace them with your strategic thinking as soon as you can. In the next few chapters we will look at how you can use similar mind set techniques to deal with injury.

CHAPTER 10

WHAT IF I
GET INJURED?

'Obstacles are those frightful things you see when you take your eyes off your goal.'

Henry Ford

I mentioned previously how I as a fat marine. Seriously, training for the marines is 9 months long and that's a long time for someone who hates fitness. The type and intensity of fitness training ramps up each week and culminates in a challenging week of Commando Test. One of which is the Tarzan Assault Course. A combination of high wire obstacles and a lung-busting assault course. During a practice run, I collapsed at the foot of a 30-foot wall. We were preparing for the

Commando phase of training which meant daily rehearsals of the tests themselves. The relentless onslaught of extreme challenges served only to make you more bruised, battered and fatigue in preparation for the test proper. The 30-foot wall was the last obstacle in the Tarzan Assault Course. Climb it and the course is done. There is a 13-minute time limit on this test. It is the shortest and most intense test of them all and the one I found most difficult. I was built more for chugging along than sprinting.

'Get up Williams!' shouted Corporal Smith, a very wiry member of our training team. He was by far the smallest trained Marine I had seen since I had arrived at the Commando Training Centre and I wondered how he had managed to haul his arse plus the 3 stone of extra battle kit up the 30-foot wall when he went through training.

'Fucking get up and crack on otherwise you fail!' He bellowed. I looked up at him and fully expected him to kick me in the gut for being pathetic, but he did quite the opposite. He crouched down so his mouth was close to my ear. 'Come on Williams' he whispered. 'If you can get this far you can get over the wall!'.

'I don't think I can Corporal" I gasped. My breathing was so erratic, it was difficult to breath and my legs throbbed with the build-up of lactic acid.

'How did you get up there Corporal... how? It seems impossible'

'I'll teach you...' he said 'First, whenever you

come across an obstacle that seems unsur-mountable point at it with one finger!'

He *is* mental I thought.

'Point at it Williams...' He shouted as he grabbed my combat jacket and shook it violently.

I lifted my weary arm and pointed at the thick, stone wall. I could see the wear of thousands of previous recruits that had scaled it before me on the small foot and hand holds.

'Now what Corporal?' I asked.

'Now notice that when you point at any obstacle and you look at your hand there are three times more fingers pointing back at you! You are the obstacle Williams... you have to conquer yourself, not the wall!'

My mind suddenly focussed inwards. I no longer scoured the wall for a route I thought I can manage, I searched myself for the tiniest resource that could help.

'Three fingers back at you Williams' Corporal Smith Shouted '...you are three times more paralysing and overwhelming than that obstacle will ever be!'

'But why put the hardest obstacle right before the finish?' I said, but deep down I could feel my state change. I was starting to look for resources I could call on to help... I was building in strength and confidence and even my breathing had calmed.

'The wall isn't just before the finish Williams you dumb fuck!!! The wall IS the finish!'

I stepped onto the wall, slowly I started to climb. I focussed on the top and took it inch by inch. Soon I was half way... three quarters up and then my hand reached the top. I pulled my self over and into the parapet. I let out an ear-piercing cheer as I had conquered my nemesis and I turned to the PTI on top for recognition of what I had achieved.

The PTI looked at me and said in a bewildered manner... 'What do you want a kiss? Get off my wall you fat fuck!'

What did I expect? I started to make my way down the ladder and caught site of Corporal Smith. He pointed at me and with the tiniest nod, I realised there was no such thing as an obstacle. Just a lack of resourcefulness.

I so desperately wanted to be a marine and constantly questioned why we would drill and run ourselves into the ground in pursuit of a green beret. I spent a lot of time worrying about the training even though I could not change it and if I was to pass it had to be done! It wasn't until I completed commando training that I realised it wasn't the green beret that made you a commando, it was the training that gave you the skills, the knowledge, the grit and the pride of being a member of the nation's elite. The training wasn't an obstacle. Training was the path. Remember there is nothing 'in' the way. Everything you are experiencing right now is 'on the way'.

With that being said, let's chat about another

prominent fear in your preparation for the MDS. Injury.

Dealing with injury

During the pre-survey of 2016 runners, injuries featured heavily, but in three main contexts. Primarily pre-existing injuries and how to deal with them. Closely followed by injury prevention during training and finally the fear of injury during the event itself.

This chapter will not give you the latest tips for using form rollers and kryo chambers to aid recovery, what I want to focus on is your mental battle with this and I have a formula for it.

We employ a happiness formula at our residential fitness camp to help people eradicate worry and genuinely beat the fear of injury or the psychological battle of recovering from injury.

The formula is simple to employ, but as with many things, can be hard to implement. My wife Paula first introduced me to the happiness formula and I immediately stole it to use not only for my coaching clients and students but also for myself. It serves as a great reminder of what to do when things go wrong.

The Happiness Formula

$E + R = O$

Phew... I can almost hear the audible sign from those with maths as crap as mine. Like I said, it is super easy to remember so let me break it down.

E (Event) – In the past...

The first part of the equation is E. It stands for Event. Now many events we simply cannot do anything about. Even ones that could have been prevented are fixed in our timeline now.

During my preparation, I picked up a virus, had a tear in my calf, IT band pain in my left leg… all of it affected my training. Of course, it would, but I never doubted that I wouldn't be ready for the MDS because I implemented the Happiness equation.

0 (Outcome) – In the future…

Hey, I jumped one! I know, I always explain it this way as I want to stress the most important part last. A little like a movie where the hero finally gets the girl. Anyway… back to it. The O (Outcome) is what we tend to concern ourselves. We can have a small tweak in our knees around mile 10 and immediately start to conjure up images of ourselves limping to the finish line in need of a total knee reconstruction. We pile on the worry and add a little more pressure on ourselves and load up our MDS worry backpack… which, you will remember from earlier in the book is far heavier than our kit backpack.

R (response) – In the now…

Finally, the R (response). Now, this is the only aspect that we can affect. We can seldom do anything about the event. We cannot change things. Even if we could have been a little more careful when running along rocky, uneven ground we cannot now change the fact we have turned an ankle. Even in our broader life, we can't go back and stop the crappy events in our lives. We can, however, change our response. I was coaching a lady recently who said she felt so lucky that she had not had any terrible things happen to her during her childhood. I asked if she had ever been bullied or can she remember a time when her family really had to rally around and help her or any other family member. Turns out she used to get pinned to the floor by the other kids at school who sat on her and called her 'a whale!' Her response was… 'oh that's nice. I love whales'. As for a time when the family had to rally together, she told me of a time when her brother had a terrible car accident and was left paralysed. She had a choice, was he to be a huge burden on her as she grew up… or was this situation a gift? They could have so easily lost him completely? Turns out her life was littered with significant experiences, but her response created her perception of them. What an amazing outlook from a very young age.

The R (Response) is the only time and factor in this equation where you can focus your energy and efforts to decide and follow through on. The Response is in the Now. It's what you do right now and the 'now' is a gift, that's why we call it the present. Your response dictates your outcome. How you respond to the little niggles and pains or even the more serious injuries will dictate your outcome.

How Are You Currently Responding?

Take a minute to think back to a negative event that happened in your training recently. The significance of the event is not important. Large or small, severe or trivial choose an event and take yourself back to that time. How did you react? What feelings and emotions did you feel during the event? Was it a time when your training session was scuppered by other peoples in ability to organise and plan? Maybe a family event got in the way? Maybe you had planned a training run only for the weather to close in? Maybe you slept in? Maybe you couldn't be arsed or you sabotaged yourself?

Now think about how you reacted. Did you fail forward or backward?

Failure is a good thing.

Failing is natural. It's how we learn. Failing causes, us to review what went wrong. If we went through life getting everything right first time we wouldn't learn a great deal. But we can either fail backwards and make decisions that do not serve us or we can fail forwards and make decisions that empower us to learn, move forward and progress. Failing forward causes us to pick out the thing that did work and ditch or alter the things that did not.

This is not the most important thing you can learn from this book.

I want to stress the importance of this mindset hack. I need you to understand the gravity of the R in this equation. It could be the difference between you finishing the MDS and a cold hard DNF next to your name on the race report. It's a great lesson for life in general too. Most people have never taken the time to check their response to events. It never occurs to them that they can control all their outcomes. They can either get the crap they have right now or create the very best result possible. It is all a choice and it is your responsibility to make the best one. Response-ability! You always have a choice and always have the ability. See?

This equation works! It stacks the power in your favour in every challenging event in your training and even your life. It releases your mindset from being at the effect of other people and other events that let's face it will always try to knock you off course. Life itself will find ways to knock you off course and push you around, but if we can shape our response. Make smarter choices over what we do and how we react, we can be happier, lighten our worry pack and lift the weight from our shoulders.

So... what have we learned? Injuries happen. We are stressing our bodies to get fitter and if we stress anything too much it will break. We all have little niggles that we will take on to the MDS, but we each have the opportunity to respond in a way we are grateful and happy with the outcome.

Pre-existing injuries

So how does this work with pre-existing injuries? Again, we cannot do anything about your pre-existing injury. You have it now, all you can do is concentrate on your reaction to it.

Here are a couple of examples from the 2016 event.

As part of the Walking with The Wounded team I got to meet Duncan Slater, a double amputee that participated in the Marathon Des Sables... What about his pre-existing injury lol? He has no friggin feet!!!

Another participant completed the event with terminal cancer... now Duncan amazed me. This guy shook my entire world! We get cancer, maybe we could have prevented it, maybe we were always destined for it... it no longer matters. The only thing that matters is that we decide to respond in a manner whereby we are content with the outcome.

For your pre-existing injury, can you rehab it? Can you find expert help to overcome it? Is it ideal that you have an injury? No... Will it mean you will not complete the MDS? Probably not if you are smart about the recovery and rehab. I see rugby league players bounce back each week having sustained ridiculous injuries during games. Your body is an amazing thing and you have no idea of its potential if you get your crazy self-defeating thoughts out of the way.

Injury prevention

Now you have released the pressure of having to cope with any existing injuries, you have the clarity and reassurance that you can find help and get the injury fixed or at least make it manageable.

In this chapter, we have explored the effect of injuries and how we can react to them. Most niggles are manageable if you are smart. It is too easy to get overwhelmed by injuries, but think about what you can do right now. What is the smallest thing you can do right now to help with this injury? Rest, ice, compression, self-massage maybe even book an appointment with a specialist. Injuries happen... *but...* they can be overcome and dealt with if your response is appropriate and positive. Keep that in mind as we move into the next chapter on blisters.

CHAPTER 11

THE B WORD

'Even with heavily blistered feet, you can still run!'

Dr Mark Stroud

No book about the MDS would be complete without broaching the subject of the B word. Blisters! Now for all the experience I have with mindset and performance coaching, it pales into insignificance compared to the experience I have with the treatment and prevention of blisters.

From the day, I started playing rugby seriously to the day I left the Marines I have suffered from foot and blister problems. My wife Paula assures me it's because of the weird, size, shape and the fallen arches in my feet which are comforting... thanks, dear! Anyway, I rapidly learnt that prevention is far greater than cure, but also treatment is far greater than leaving them and suffering.

A blister is caused by friction against the upper layers of skin. Our body then fills the pockets with water a protective measure, but the friction and damage to the skin are painful. Sometimes even the smallest blister can be crippling. During the selection process from special forces, I lost all the skin on the back of my heal. The tendon sheaths were pretty much exposed and the whole of my Achilles was a weeping mess of raw skin. Each morning I would peel my feet from the bed sheets. Bath and dress them, pop a couple of paracetamol before heading out for long route marches and even swims in the sea... which was cute, to say the least!

I must say at this point that although I didn't let the DocTrotters anywhere near my feet, they do an amazing job. In fact, the entire support staff, especially the medical staff, are tremendous during the MDS. I never went to the DocTrotters because A - I would rather have a camel dry hump my head than let someone else touch my feet, I had the experience and equipment to treat my own and I would rather be refuelling and rehydrating in my tent than queuing for a painful and traumatic experience. Seriously, I cannot speak highly enough of the medical team. Incidentally, I did take comfort in the heartless doctor stand-off that took place when our very own GP (Generally Pissed-off) doctor Pete went for his feet dressing.

Prevention of blisters is centred around reducing friction or conditioning the skin to abrasion. What I will say is you may be the lucky one that doesn't suffer from blisters and some people go through the MDS without picking up any blisters, but many people also suffer. My take on this is you probably know if you tend to suffer from blisters and your training runs and events will highlight this or not. If not you do not know if you will be one of the few that escape blisters while crossing the desert so I would recommend the following.

Before

Test your trainers and socks over a greater distance and over the tough wet terrain. Thus, will allow you to identify potential hot spots and troublesome areas for protection later, but also help condition your feet to the extra battering they will receive in the desert. Conditioning your feet should form part of your preparation and doesn't take a great deal of effort.

Learn some basic taping techniques which will enable you to protect your feet sufficiently. You can watch my videos at RunningLightBook. com/Resources

Be wary of apparent 'cure-alls'. I have not tried all the blister prevention products and ointments out there but would be very wary of many.

Stock up on zinc oxide tape of both 2" and 1" in diameter for use during training and in the race itself.

During

Check your socks and footwear for any potentially abrasive edges, excessive threading or components of the shoe that could cause increased rubbing on the feet.

Keep your feet as dry and clean as possible and allow them to air at the start and end of every day.

Tape your troublesome areas each day and inspect your feet at the end of each day for new hot spots or for taping that needs replacing. I would recommend you only remove and replace tape that is visibly damaged, getting quite manky or has proved to be ineffective.

Treat and dress and blisters that require attention (see below), keep clean and allow to air overnight before dressing and re-taping in the morning.

Be careful not to disturb or roll up the edges of the tape as you put your socks on.

If hot spots or blisters develop along the route, take a few minutes to treat and protect them to maintain a more consistent and less painful pace for the rest of the day / event. Far better to stop to 'sharpen the axe' than spend many extra painful hours struggling through.

After

Stick to a regular treatment plan with regular antiseptic bathing, cleaning and re-dressing blisters to prevent infection. Your blisters will heal best when allowed to dry out. The body dries out the lower layers of skin to form outer skin. It is a natural process that will be hindered with too many lotions and excessive dressing.

Treatment

Once again you can watch videos and treatment guides for blisters at RunningLightBook. com/resources until then I would recommend the following treatment of blisters.

Hot spots

Hot spots form before a blister emerges. They are the early signs and symptoms of a deeper, more advanced blister. Failing to treat a hot spot will result in a more painful and difficult to treat blister. As soon as you feel the onset of a hot spot STOP and treat.

Hot spots are relatively easy to treat with a little tape or if you are close to the end of the run with some anti-chafing gel or Vaseline, tough ointments rarely last more than a few miles. In theory sounds easy, but in practice, my experience has shown that it is challenging to get the tape to stick to wet or sweaty skin. During the MDS I would recommend drying the area with your buff and allow it time to air for a while to dry out before applying tape. Rub the tape vigorously with the palm of your hand to warm the adhesive glue and ensure the tape lasts as long as possible. As always, avoid rolling the corners and edges of the tape as you replace your sock and trainer.

Superficial blisters (not burst)

There are two types of people in the world when it comes to blisters. None poppers and poppers!!! The none-poppers are right. The cleanest and the best way to treat a blister that has bubbled up is to leave the skin intact, air and allow the body's natural healing process to take effect.

However, the none poppers are not midway through the toughest foot race on earth and do not have the down time to do that, but can also do without a blister tearing open exposing untreated raw skin halfway through the sand dunes. Painful!

I would recommend popping your blisters with a sterile needle. Create a hole at the uppermost part of the blister to allow air in and create a separate draining hole at the bottom. Gently squeeze the fluid out and be aware that because blisters form as layers of skin separate and we have 5 layers of skin in the upper part of skin we can have blisters on blisters sometimes. In this case, I would attempt to drain both. I wouldn't go digging too much if I couldn't get to the deepest blister, though.

After draining the blister cut away as much of the free skin as possible. Treat with antiseptic, protect against dirt and allow the raw skin to air overnight before applying a protective dressing such as Granuflex®, Second Skin® or even a thin medical dressing before taping securely.

Superficial blisters (burst)

Usually the most painful stage of a blister, the torn skin exposes a very raw, tender and painful inner layer which hurts like hell, but the good news is the bursting has been done for you. Every cloud and all that... cut away and free skin and treat as above.

Removing the skin is important because it can dry and form hard slithers of skin which can dig into tender areas and therefore are best removed.

Blisters and friction burns on other areas of the body

Other potentially troublesome areas are anywhere where kit and clothing will rub excessively. Upper and lower back, shoulders and hips from the backpack, nipples, crotch and even the end of your winkle... gents obviously! Ladies, you think you have it bad with period pains and childbirth... try friction burns on the little fella!!! #Trauma!

Same rules apply though it is unlikely you will get watery blisters like you do on your feet. Other areas of the body tend to suffer from friction wearing away the skin. Check kit, test, test, test and protect with tape as required and don't think it's weird to ask your wife to shave your back and apply tape before you leave for Morocco. Just have an If-Then statement for getting stopped at customs like I did with strange and very large strips of tape across your back and little bags of white powder in your hand luggage. They didn't know whether I was a bomber or a drug mule, but eventually I explained what they tape was for and that the powder was a recovery shake.

During my service, I learnt that the pain and discomfort from blisters can be handled by the body and paracetamol is about the most effective and easily accessible drug to take the edge from the pain. Be sure to stick to the suggested dose, use the techniques above and then remember that the body will produce numbing chemicals once you get started. You just have to get started in the morning and avoid stopping for too long for the rest of the day. See Tony's interview later in the book for evidence of that.

In this chapter, we have explored the prevention, treatment and management of blisters. Prevention is always more favourable than treatment and management so I suggest you are proactive in protecting the feet. Better to complete the race with taped feet and no blisters rather than take a chance, not tape up and potentially suffer. In the next few chapters we will go deeper into your fitness and preparation physically.

PART 2

CHAPTER 12

FITNESS
(ESTIMATED 20% OF YOUR MDS SUCCESS)

I stepped out of the house with tired eyes. It was a crisp winter's morning with a perfectly clear sky. I looked at the stars as I fitted my Bluetooth headphones and selected an audiobook to listen to. I fumbled with my head torch for a few seconds more than I expected as it was new and turning it on was not obvious. After cycling through no light, high beam 'burn your retina out' light and red flashing light, I managed to set it to an illumination level I was happy with. I sucked a lung full of crisp air in through my nose and stepped off. In terms of setting myself up for success this morning, I had played an absolute blinder! It had all started the night before by preparing it all. I had even slept in my shorts and t-shirt so I wouldn't have to stumble around the bedroom and wake my wife. My socks, trainers and windproof outer jacket were waiting at the back door like a little puppy anxious to go for a walk. It struck me how I had neglected them over the last few months. I had prepped a small running belt with two 250 ml bottles of water and snacks. My phone and headphones were charged and my head torch hung from the back-door handle. I'm normally an early riser but early morning exercise is not my thing. I prefer to train later in the day when I have more energy, but that was allowing life to get in the way and as willpower and motivation diminished as the day wore on... something had to change. Normally I spend the early mornings writing or working, but with the MDS rapidly approaching, I had to get my arse in gear. I wanted to start the day with a huge win and had planned a 20-mile route that strategically avoided any potential for shortcuts. The route I chose meant that once I hit the halfway point there really was no point even turning back, I was committed to a 20-mile run. It was a perfect demonstration of everything I had learnt from years of sedentary people breaking into exercise.

I felt light on my feet. I was running down the dotted white line of the dark country roads in Lincolnshire and I was surprised to notice just how good this felt. I felt free and very happy. I even did a couple of pirouettes within the first mile. I really had missed this. Suddenly something caught my attention. A small, rugby ball shaped white form in my periphery. Turning my head, the light from the head torch illuminated a barn owl watching me from his perch in a tree. 'Wow!' I thought. A couple of hundred meters down the road and a fox darted across the road and two miles further, I came across a badger working his way through the leaf litter looking for worms and other insects to eat.

Whenever I ran, I am reminded of a phrase a good friend told me. He was a great runner with a 2:40 London marathon time. 'Make the most of the easy miles' he would say. These were definitely easy miles and I was showing little sign of slowing. My legs felt relatively strong and I enjoyed the pieces of parmesan and chorizo I was trialling for the MDS. Checking my watch, I was surprised to learn I was just short of 5 mins ahead of my anticipated pace as I passed RAF Cosford, a nearby military camp that I had noted as my halfway mark. My mind was clear and even my feet, that had suffered terribly with blisters over the years were holding up.

'Shit!!!' I said out loud as I started a moderate incline at about mile 14. My legs seemed drained. Where had the happy, light-footed skip that I started with gone? I instantly regretted the pirouettes from earlier. 'If only I'd saved more energy earlier on instead of auditioning for Strictly in front of the counties Wildlife, I'd be coping better with this hill!' I slowed my stride and broke into a walk. I kidded myself by swinging my arms and striding out, but this was obviously the beginning of the end. Everything from that point on could only be described as laboured! My breathing, cadence, stride pattern, but more importantly my internal dialogue was hard fucking work! I topped up my blood sugar with some jelly sweets and sipped on some of the cool refreshing water, but the boost was only temporary.

I struggled through the next 2 miles, the amount of traffic was increasing as Lincolnshire slowly came to life, but this only added to my misery. Each time a vehicle passed, I had to leap from the roadside onto the verge for safety. It broke up my already disrupted stride pattern and I was getting infused by the speeding commuters. The truth was it wasn't their fault I felt like this! I had failed to keep up with my training, had allowed other aspects of life to take priority.

Despite years of developing an unwavering Commando Spirit, I called my wife for a pickup. I felt relieved. There was no denying my energy was heavily depleted. I had not made the full transition to running on fats and my hypogly-caemic state felt horrendous.

After the phone call I never even tried to break into a jog again. For what seemed like an age I plodded along so I didn't freeze in the morning frost. The relief was immense as I saw Paula's car appear and slow to pick me up. I love my wife completely, but my love for her doubled as she pulled up to rescue me. We were both silent as I opened the door and got in. We didn't speak a word the whole way back to the house. She instinctively knew that was not the time to ask what went wrong.

As I slumped down into Paula's passenger seat, aching, nauseous, and dejected I was not only geographically, but also metaphorically miles from the skipping running lover that set off this morning... My mind flashed to the MDS and at that point, I realised I was physically way out of my depth!

By rights, this fitness chapter should be the easiest section for me to write. Honestly, I'm quite reluctant to write it. My editor suggested it would be an essential part of the completed book, so here goes. My reluctance comes from seeing way too many fitness professionals muddying the waters during my prep for the race. I don't want to add to it. 'Train like this', 'train like that', 'this worked for me...'. The problem is that sometimes even the best-laid plans are disrupted by life. Plans and programmes are fantastic and I love deadlines too...! I love the sound they make as they whizz by! I know this all too well. My training programme quickly went to rat shit within a few weeks of starting it.

Almost immediately after being granted a place by the Walking With The Wounded charity I laid out my training programme for the next 16 months. Despite being hugely 'towards motivated' I started well. I put a blog together to track my progress and started with weekly update videos and posts about how training was going. Soon after, however, it ground to a halt. Life threw too many curveballs. Home and business life got in the way of my intention of training consistently for the whole period before the event.

So, in this section, I'll speak about some of the obvious fitness mistakes I and others made. I will also outline the strategies I used to prepare for the MDS after I realised my fitness was woefully inadequate. It seems funny now that the 4-week panic training phase I went through just before we flew to Morocco actually included 2 weeks of tapering... would you believe it? lol.

First up let's get clear on the importance of fitness in your attempt at the MDS. How much of a factor does it play? During my survey, it was clear that fitness was the biggest worry for most people and it was obviously also the number 1 factor people focused on. It's like Marines training where beforehand you think fitness will be 50% of what makes up the challenge. Actually, I suggest it is much smaller than that as I outlined above. Trust me on one thing, your head will give in way before your body ever will. I believe the fitness will be 20% of whether you succeed in the MDS or not. Now fitness should definitely not be left to chance, time can be invested better than just treading miles and miles at a moderate pace or stressing out because you couldn't get the 2 hours needed to do the long run together. I base much of my opinion on the fact I completed the race despite being considerably out of condition.

Running with anchors

Imagine sitting in a classroom and the teacher suddenly scrapes his nails down the chalkboard! In fact, take a second now and think about your mobile. Who, when they call, creates a feeling of impending doom when you see their names on the screen? Maybe you have a couple of friends or relatives that when you see them calling, you think 'Oh no... not now'?

These reactions are what we call 'anchors'. We have anchored an emotional state those sites and sounds. Anchors also work with smells, feelings and tastes too. Do you have certain perfumes or aftershaves that take you back to that first love? Songs that remind you of certain periods of your life such as holidays or parties? What about the smell of orange or cinnamon and Christmas? What thoughts and feelings are triggered by the Coca-Cola trucks and the 'holidays are coming' advert?

Maybe you haven't really thought about these triggers before, but the truth is we develop anchors for all kinds of things that we receive through our senses including Visual, Auditory, Kinaesthetic, Olfactory and Gustatory or VAKOG for short.

- Visual - The things we see
- Auditory - Sounds
- Kinaesthetic - Feelings and touch
- Olfactory - Smell
- Gustatory - Taste

NLP practitioners have been using anchors for decades to recreate or orchestrate optimal states to help us. Right now, I am sat writing with specialist background music playing as a scented candle burns. These are some of the triggers I use to generate a fastidious and focused typing state within the body. I call these my success initiators because whenever I create this signals for my sense I become very focused.

Following the disastrous run above I created a different anchor for the MDS. With a relatively simple NLP technique, I created a determination anchor on the face of my watch. Whenever I start to feel tired, fed up of running or a lack of motivation I press my left thumb against the face of my Suunto watch. Through a simple process, I have installed and can now trigger a deep feeling of determination at will. It may sound weird to you at first but I have seen people successfully use anchors to conquer a fear of public speaking, generate enough confidence to break free from an abusive partner, control bouts of uncontrollable aggression during rugby games at the highest level and much more. Ever seen Jonny Wilkinson prepare for a conversion?

Installing an anchor

Installing an anchor is relatively easy and though is easier installed by someone else, can be created on your own. Timing is essential.

Before we start. Think about what state would suit you when running? Maybe you lack a little determination? Perhaps you're fine once you get going, but lack the motivation sometimes? Are you nervous running downhill or in the dark and would benefit from a courage anchor? Are you plagued by silly, uncontrollable race day strategies and focus or decisiveness would help? In contrast, do you take things way too serious and you need to relax or lighten up sometimes?

Think about what strength you would love to be able to summon at will. If you cannot think of one, that's fine. Just think, if you could think of one what would it be?

Now select an area on your body where you will have easy access when running and that will not be triggered by accident. No point having a killer finish, 'get out of my way mother Hubbard's... I'm coming through!' anchor on your elbow where it can be triggered as you jostle for position on the start line. Usually, pressing a knuckle, touching a watch face, rotating a ring around your finger, holding a pendant or even forming a tight fist are good places to start.

Ok, now you have chosen both the desired state and where you want to install the anchor we will go through a simple process to create it. There are many advanced ways to do this which I cover in our mindset coaching days, but this technique is a great place to start.

The process is simple. We recreate the desired state in our body and as the feeling builds we press the spot, twist the ring, wiggle your woggle, (do the Macarena!) or do whatever it is you decided would be the trigger. Hold it until the feeling starts to dissipate or for a maximum of 5-6 seconds then release it. Repeat that process three times and you are done!

Read through all the steps below before carrying out the complete process.

- Step 1 - Say your desired state out loud.

- Step 2 - Think of a time in your life when you truly felt your desired state. Think about all the feelings you felt, sounds your heard, sights you saw that time when you truly felt your desired state.

- Press and hold the anchor as the feeling is generated in your body. As the feeling dissipates or for a maximum of 5-6 seconds release it.

- Step 3 - How many light bulbs can you see right now? Say the answer out loud. Step 3 is what we call a 'break state'. The feelings generated by step 2 can hang around unless we clear our mind with another thought.

- Step 4 - Repeat step 2 with a different memory.

- Step 5 - Break state... How many vowels are in this sentence? Say the answer out loud.

- Step 6 - Repeat step 2 with one last memory.

- Step 7 - Carry out a final break state... What make was the last pair of running trainers you purchased? Say the answer out loud.

- Step 8 - Test the anchor!!!

You will get the makings of your desired state building inside you. You will probably be nodding your head a little as you think about it. That's right... now the good thing about anchors is they are an inexhaustible resource. In fact, every time they are triggered they get stronger and stronger.

The power of an anchor

Alice arrived at TEAM Bootcamp from Nigeria. Like so many of the clients that come to us to tackle weight and fitness issues, her issues were much deeper than just overeating. After a lifetime of bullying, Alice felt worthless and was petrified of even sitting in the same room as strangers. Alice was one of the tallest women I had ever seen. She dwarfed me (which isn't hard!!!) and looked like a warrior with her stature. Despite some deep-rooted feelings, Alice was an easy nut to crack. As a team, we had discussed her lack of confidence and allowed her to integrate at their own pace for the first week. Then during a mindset coaching session, I could see that something I had said or done sparked something inside her. Though Alice usually had a veiled look on her face, fearing that any emotion may betray her, she smiled and in that split second, I pressed my finger onto her fifth knuckle. I am not sure how long it had been since a man had touched her. In fact, I wonder if a white man had touched her at all?

'Take this gift Alice' I said as I pressed firmly onto her knuckle. 'It's a confidence anchor and every time you press it, you will feel confidence radiate through your body!'

She smiled and everyone in the room cheered. Throughout the rest of the session, I would periodically press the anchor. She smiled... the room cheered! After the session, I encouraged all the other campers to use the confidence anchor on Alice each time they got the chance. Alice went on to become one of the greatest clients we have ever had. Every long-term client that stays with us for more than 12 weeks at a time receives a graduation night. It's a small celebration of their achievement. We put the equivalent weight Alice had lost into a backpack and asked her to pick it up. She couldn't!!! She had scorched more than 60kg in 12 weeks but left a beautiful, proud and almost stoic woman. She returns this year for a 3 week top up. We cannot wait to see her again.

The three mental stages of any ultra-leg.

Now before we start with this section, have you ever thought about how you would eat an elephant? It may sound like a crazy question, but when you think about it, eating an elephant is a huge challenge that would take a few days, probably a bit of pain or discomfort and something that if you attempted it... other people would think 'What the f...?!'

Well, the answer is one bite at a time. It really is as simple as that and so is any challenge we face in life. Thinking about eating the whole thing in one go is too overwhelming. Like the lion tamer earlier, remember?

I asked lots of runners how they broke the long distances down into manageable chunks and although the race is broken down geographically, few had any psychological milestones of their own. I developed psychological milestones that helped me set my pace, structure my eating and drinking, but also helped me avoid overwhelm during the race.

I broke the running day into three psychological stages:

1. Easy out
2. Jockey for position
3. Live to fight another day

The easy out stage was a reminder at the start of each day to not get carried away. I recovered extremely well each day and tended to run too hard and too fast at the start and I learnt from day 1, checkpoint 1 that the desert will give me a good hard kick in the nuts if I didn't respect it during the first few legs of the day. It did not mean dawdle during the first legs. My definition of easy out meant that I would hold back slightly and not worry if others passed me or seemed to be moving considerably faster than I did. I would just let them go and stick to my own pace, knowing that stage 2 would soon follow.

Stage 2, jockey for position, was extremely motivating and after a relatively slow start, I found

I had the energy to spare. So instead of being caught and overtaken by others or constantly passing, being overtaken, passing, being overtaken by the same people, I now found that I was moving much quicker than the others around me. It was a huge psychological boost to the middle and later stages of the day. This was usually quite a mundane time of the day, but the 'jockey for position' strategy helped me break up the monotony.

The final psychological milestone to every day was to live to fight another day. Within the last stage of the race I would ease back into a race pace I was relatively happy with and begin my recovery for the next day. At a point where I was happy with the number of other runners I had picked off, I would settle into a gap between two runners moving at roughly the same pace as me. For me, this was often the hottest part of the day and a wise time to slow a little, maintain hydration and have a metaphorical margin for a short break in the shade or slightly extended water break at a checkpoint. Each day, each leg, each step was just another bite of the elephant.

Run v's walk

I think lots of regular club runners with limited to moderate experience in marathons were surprised with the amount of walking the environment and accumulation of fatigue forced them to do. It seems weird that you could struggle with going too slow, but it happened. I think lots of people spent a lot of time training at around or slightly below their regular running pace but failed to spend any real-time hiking for extended periods. I suppose as a runner, walking seems laborious and... well... slow!!! Nevertheless, the soft sand, heat, fatigue, dehydration, blisters, injuries and many other aspects forced participants to walk. I know this frustrated people that wanted to be moving faster than the terrain allowed. Many people were slaves to their GPS watches which piled a lot of pressure onto them. I met one guy that said his watch had died in the first few days of the race, but he felt less pressure now he wasn't running against the little ghost image of himself on a screen.

So how did I know when to run and when to walk? The final test for the Royal Marines is a 30-mile route march carrying a minimum of 22lbs of kit and your rifle. It comes at the end of 30+ weeks of tough military training and is the culmination of the Commando Course. A gruelling battle hardening period that originated during world war two and is designed to not just test the suitability of a Royal Marine for the elite forces, but also to forge the heart and mind of a Commando! All in all, the Commando Course is a multi-stage endurance event over challenging terrain. The 30-Miler takes place on Dartmoor and no matter what the weather two things are guaranteed, you will get a frozen pasty as your 'race nutrition' and it is happening! There is a strict time limit on the event regardless of how wet, cold, hot or stormy the weather conditions are. For my 30-miler I was lucky. The weather was pretty none descript even though it had rained heavily a few days before and the ground was waterlogged in places, the prevailing weather was perfect.

Now the thing with the 30-miler is you simply cannot run it all. First up, you are running as a squad and although everyone has their personal kit allocation to carry, two safety Bergen's of up to 40lbs are passed between the squad. You must move at the pace of the slowest people and quickly settle into a system of jogging the downhills and flats, but marching up hill and over tricky terrain. The MDS was the same. Few people could run the whole event. Even the elite runners were forced to walk a couple of the rocky ridges and steep, soft sand inclines. Not many of them, but some! So, for us mortal runners it's a case of walking much of the route and running when you can, not expecting to run most of the route and walking when you must.

Ok you may feel differently during your training and believe that you will run most of the route, but pretty much everyone I spoke to that finished the race greater than 150 in the race order were surprised at just how much walking they did.

A mile in someone else's steps

Another aspect of desert running that seems counterintuitive is walking in other people's footprints. I quickly learnt to hunt out the on touched, virgin sand in the dunes. It seemed to take my weight better and I got more propulsion than walking where others had broken the sand. At first, I thought that the sand in people's footprints would be more stable than untouched sand, but it wasn't. I think this idea originated from walking in deep snow where you seek out the footprints and tracks of others to make movement easier. It's different in sand. I think I kidded myself that there was no way the sand in the Sahara could be anything like the sand on the Scarborough beach where walking was laboured and running was hard! Well it was, it is and for you... it will be!

...But... it doesn't have to be fast and it doesn't have to be pretty... it just needs to be done! Stay with the bow wave!

Running circles around the desert.

This seems like an ideal place to remind you about concentrating on the circles of influence and disregarding the circles of concern. Later in this book in an interview with top performance coach Phil Quirk, we introduce Stephen Covey's theory of two circles. A circle that contains all the factors that you can do feck all about like the weather, the terrain, other people and your penis size (sorry that last one was just for me!). We call this the circle of concern. Thinking about these factors are pointless and frustrating. There is nothing we can do about them. The second circle is the circle of influence. Conversely, we control everything within the circle from our attitude, nutrition, hydration, protection from the elements, kit rubbing, blisters and much more.

I want to plant the seed that IF you feel overwhelmed, frustrated, confused, under pressure, whether it be self-imposed or other or any other emotion that does not empower you THEN check which circle you are working in. Forget the concerns. Why beat yourself up and bully yourself with things you can do nothing about and focus instead on the things you can influence and change or do more of. It'll get you out of a rut and move again, or in this case potentially out of the soft sand and onto firm ground where you can make better progress again.

Compression wear

Just a quick note on running with compression wear. There isn't a great deal of evidence to suggest that running with compression wear will enhance your performance and personally I hate it, but if it works for you, go for it. Just remember compression gear is a tactic not a strategy and strategies always beat tactics.

I did take compression tights on the MDS but more to aid recovery at the end of each day.

Finally!

The last thing I want to pass on in this chapter is a reminder of running technique and style. With all endurance events, we can burn up a lot of energy by holding redundant muscles and muscle groups tense. Often, I see people running with fixed feet, hands, shoulders, arms and probably the most frequent, clenched fists. Each isometric hold throughout the body is consuming vital energy stored within the body or that could be used elsewhere. A common IF THEN statement of mine was to run relaxed. At every opportunity, I would complete the following checks throughout my body:

- Hands - Shake out my hands and fingers. Can I feel the cooling effect of the wind between my fingers?

- Wrists - Are my wrists limp and lower than my waist?

- Elbows - Are my elbows half-cocked and relaxed?

- Shoulders - Am I holding my shoulders tight or are they relaxed. If not, allow them to drop and pull them back slightly to remove any pressure on the neck.

- Breathing and chest - Am I breathing freely using both my belly and rib cage to inhale. Is it easier to breathe with my mouth open? Personally, I think the whole 'in through you nose out of your mouth' is bull shit. Why the hell would we try to counter the amount of air and oxygen our body needs? It's a bit arrogant to think we know better than the signals our autonomous nervous system receives. Remember, breathing capacity and rate increases during exercise because we need to get rid of the waste, not because we need more oxygen. Just allow your body to breath naturally... as in, how it wants to! If that's in through the mouth and out for the arse then let it!

- Trunk - Lean forward slightly on the downhills. Let gravity help.

- Legs - Soften the legs slightly especially the shins and ankles. Relax!

Day end strategies.

I mentioned before that I tended to start the day in much better wear than many of the other runners which I put down to the 'live another day' technique and a strict end of day recovery strategy.

Ok... so first things first. Smile and blow a kiss at the finish line webcam (try to look strong), grab my super sweet, sugar laced green tea, juggle the extra water bottles they pile into your arms and limp to tent (which feels like it is getting further and further from the finish each day), collapse for 5 mins (minimum) before preceding to expel all remnants of the aforementioned green tea from my stomach through Exorcist-esque vomiting and always in that order!

Once complete begin self-recovery regime.

Having cleared any large stones from around the tent and seriously placing them under Pete's part of the dusty, noodle stained rug we called a mattress I would settle down to sorting my feet, food, first aid and fuel.

I have never smoked or taken drugs, but I guess the first fag... (no wait... I should write cigarette to avoid confusion!) after sex is the closest you can get to the feeling of taking your trainers after a stage of the MDS!

FEET - First up in my regime is to get my trainers off and get some air around my toes

FOOD - Start to prepare food. If you take a stove or blocks of solid fuel, set it all up now and get it cooking in the sun. Make up your recovery shake (unless you drank it in the last 5k of your run) and eat a couple of small snacks to prevent massive fluctuation in your blood sugar. Being either hypoglycaemic (low blood sugar) or hyper-glycaemic (high blood sugar) can make you very ill following a long endurance event.

FIRST AID - A little self-love goes a long way here... no, I don't mean start masturbating in the middle of the bivouac but spend a little time rubbing and massaging your feet and legs. Get the blood flowing, manipulate the toes a little and check for blisters or hot spots. I treat any blisters that need attention immediately to primarily prevent infection, but also because blisters feel a lot better even with a little basic treatment. Stretch calves, hamstrings and lower back before elevating the feet for a few mins.

FUEL - Finally I will put my compression pants on then sit back, relax... eat slowly. I got into the habit of watching for my tent mates or other people I knew returning, all the while reflecting on the day.

After eating, I'll stretch and massage tight areas more and also take care of anything else that needs a little more attention such as repairing clothing or readjusting kit.

The rest of the evening is reserved for hydrating and snacking before settling down to sleep. Remember that sleeping is healing! I stay calm while I am in the tent and watch others. It's usually those that are constantly fiddling with things that develop into absolute tent rhinos! They scratch around at things in a disorganised manner, end up losing the spoon and kick their boiling water over their sleeping bag as they pack and repack their bag. There is no place for complexity here. Keep it super simple.

Visit RunningLightBook.com/resources for videos on fitness and fitness training.

You will discover answers to the following:

- How just running and too much running are counterproductive for desert running.

- How and why you should avoid training in the 'hole'.

- How and why you should be training other components of fitness.

- How to utilise every energy system in the body.

- How to rapidly adapt to carrying weight and avoid injury without doing extra training sessions.

- Why walking could be your biggest ally in the desert.

- Learn one counter-intuitive training protocol which will set you apart in the sand dunes.

- How to condition the feet for a 270k battering.

- How to prepare the body, recruit often underutilised muscles (and some of the biggest and strongest!) for more pace and power.

In this chapter, we started with the idea of working on other aspects that help your fitness including race day preparation, strategies and what to focus on during the race. In the next chapter, we will look at your desert running food.

PART 3

CHAPTER 13

FOOD
(ESTIMATED 10% OF YOUR MDS SUCCESS)

Have ever been Hangry? You know... angry because you are hungry. Mad eh? I always see a lot of Hangry people outside Gregg's (other suppliers of shit food are available). They are so fired up on sugar withdrawals and a lack of starchy carbs that they pull the arm from a passing granny to beat the lady behind the counter for a pasty or a sandwich. Imagine having hangry episodes in the desert? It happens and in this chapter, I'll explain not only how to avoid irrational food orientated states, but also why.

I should explain that, like an increasing number of participants, I completed the MDS running predominantly on fats, not sugars like the majority. I'm not the food police, a nut job conspiracy theorist or left-wing hippy who wants the world to live on ethically sourced lentils. I just want you to have the best MDS possible for you. The benefits to running predominantly on fats to me were huge. They included having to carry less food for the same calorific hit, more taste, less emotional ups and downs and I saved a fair amount of money.

I want to plant a little seed about food and your nutrition decisions and that is there is no need to worry about food. Did you know that even the leanest human body has enough stored energy to fuel it for about 8 weeks? I think that is incredible. That said, each of us can complete the MDS without eating at all during the event! Of course, you wouldn't want to, you would feel rotten, but it does dispel some of the beliefs that people hold.

I have met lots of people both runners and non-runners (if there is such a thing?) that make statements like; 'I can't possibly go for more than a few hours without eating', 'I need to consume 2 energy gels per hour' and much more, but science has shown that those statements are not fact. They are a choice. A decision we attach a lot of gravity to and that we could potentially use as an excuse, but a choice none-the-less. We all know that decisions can be changed. Remember that we need faith as the final ingredient for optimal performance. What faith can you take from statements like; 'I can't possibly go for more than a few hours without eating' or 'I need to consume 2 energy gels per hour'?

Not a great deal. How much faith will you take from 'Regardless of what happens, I have enough stored energy to last 8 weeks'. I would argue much more. This is important because I spent the first 3 days of the MDS with absolutely no appetite. Others lost snacks and meals along the route and their heads were mashed. Fundamentally that's not ideal, but you can deal with it.

I'm not saying it would be a pleasant way to run a race, but then who knows? The human body is a phenomenal thing, but it does serve as a reminder to lighten up about the food. Make quick decisions about it based on your experience and intuition and move on to more important aspects like carving the mind of a winner.

So, I want to share my race food strategy as an option. It really makes sense to me and you may have other ideas and that's fine.

My overarching strategy was to fuel much of my work on fats. I will outline how I did it below along with the reasons why. As always, I do not intend to dig up loads of scientific research to back this up, but I do want you to know that every week we put up to 25 people through a 6-day intensive fitness regime that pushes them to their physical and emotional limits. Sound like a multi-stage ultra? We witnessed a significant change in both fluctuations in emotions and 'hunger' (withdrawals) and endurance when we changed from a low-fat nutrition plan to a high fat, moderate protein diet.

I think we often fall foul of modelling our heroes which is a great strategy unless your genetic make-up and conditioning is different. Many of the elite runners can run a sub-2:15 / 2:30 marathon and will be out on the MDS course for a considerably shorter period to you and me. The human body can store a couple of hours of glycogen in the muscles, liver and in the bloodstream and for an elite athlete a couple of energy gels are enough to fuel their performance for the whole event. Think about the game duration of other sports too, football, rugby, hockey or netball. In the case of the MDS they can probably get away with a few gels, some nuts and seeds and protein bars or energy drinks. So, we can easily think 'great. I'm out for a little longer so I will just increase the number of high carb snacks and drinks that I take'. Now at some point, the glycogen levels in the body, particularly stored within the liver will run out and the body will make a transition to run on fats and it is awkward. It feels horrible. We hit the wall, crash, whatever you want to call it. This will happen and if you have experienced it before you will know what I am talking about.

I wanted to avoid getting anywhere near the wall. The wall can get stuffed! The dunes were enough for me without having to scale a wall, whether it be metaphorical, hypothetical, physical or otherwise!

Now I know you maybe a little sceptical, well you would be. You have had years of bullshit fed to you by nutrition companies that want you to buy their products. I don't have a nutrition company, I have no hidden agenda. I bought most of my food from Poundland and over exceeded my expectations in the race.

I met a good number of sceptics in my Running Light Presentations both before and after the MDS. The stare at me with a raised eyebrow and a suspicious look on their faces. 'Surely you should run on slow release carbs?' They say. You may even be thinking the same now? 'Like what?' I ask... at that point I get answers such as, 'well pasta, rice, porridge...'. None of which are particularly slow releasing especially in the form we eat them in dehydrated expeditionary foods. They are 'slower' releasing compared to treacle or sugar but are still incredibly insulin spiking and cause violent peaks and troughs in blood sugar levels. The excessive variation in blood sugar levels makes our fuel supply inconsistent, difficult to control and mood swings erratic.

Human beings have evolved to run on fat. Only recently (the last 10,000 years) have we started to live predominantly on sugars and refined carbohydrates. They were all very hard to come by back in the day... and I mean the day, day... not the day when Kanye West was a nipper or pre-tinterweb. When we were trotting around the primitive world and every meal time was an adventure! We would supplement a moderate protein, high-fat diet with plant-based foods from vegetables to bark and occasionally seasonal fruits and if we were willing to face potential death... some honey as and when.

Leverage your on-board fuel efficiency system

You may or not know that we have two main energy systems in the human body. The Oxidative system involves fat and oxygen, is often called the aerobic system and is used for long endurance activities of low intensity. The second often known as the Anaerobic system is responsible for fuelling shorter bursts of moderate to high-intensity activity, called the glycolytic system. Finally, the Creatine Phosphate (CP) system for high to extremely high intensity, powerful movements such as jumping, sprinting and lifting sub maximal weights.

To understand these systems better, think about cars. The aerobic system would be your motorway cruising, high-efficiency diesel saloon. The CP system would be best compared to a petrol executive car that is quicker, but less efficient than the diesel. The CP system would by your sports car fuelled on nitrous oxide. Capable of extremely fast and powerful blasts, but only for short periods.

Contrary to popular belief, the body uses all three energy systems at any one time. What changes with the intensity levels is the percentage of a specific energy type? This is the reason the 'fat-burning' zone is a myth, but also the reason why a pure fat plan for the MDS is not a good idea. You would 100% have the fuel and ability to chug along for 100's of miles throughout the week, but steep hills and soft sand would not be pleasant.

So, would you expect to do a 500-mile journey along the motorway using nitrous oxide? Or is running on petrol the most efficient fuel system? Hopefully you are getting the picture.

Anyway, don't take my word for it. Successful people analyse and unsuccessful people criticise. Check it out and make your own mind up and personally I believe the whole endurance world is on the verge of switching to a higher fat fuel plan. It may take 5 or 6 years, but it will happen. We just must get past the big marketing budgets.

MDS food foundations

I recommend you use the following to help with your selection of food. Cascade down the must, should, could and would criteria below:

1. Must - Meet the race criteria

2. Should - Fuel your energy expenditure

3. Could - Send the consistent information to your body including insulin and other hormone control and taste

4. Would - Avoid any potential for sickness and or diarrhoea

Must - Meet the race criteria

The strict race criteria states that:

Each entrant must provide his/her own food (For the event duration. Inc. of admin day). He/she must select the type of food best suited to his/her personal needs, health, weather conditions, weight and backpack conditions. Each competitor must have 14,000 k/calories, that is to say, a minimum of 2,000 k/calories per day. (Courtesy of marathondessabes.co.uk website)

This is non-negotiable if you want to participate. Remember that 2,400 calories can add up in size and weight which is another reason to opt for fat based food. Carbohydrates hold 4 calories per gram whereas fat contains 9 calories per gram. Big difference in calorie to weight ratio as well as size.

Personally, I ended up with about 2,400 Cal per day and I am a medium to chubby male around 5'8" and a number of calories (in the form) I took was more than enough. In fact, I only ate half my daily allowance for the first 3 days as the heat and exertion kicked my appetite well and truly out of me.

Should - Fuel your past, present & future energy expenditure

Today's food is yesterday's and tomorrow's fuel. It's easy to only concern yourself with what's coming up the next day during a multi-stage race, but we need to replace the fuel we consumed yesterday or throughout the today AND create an excess for the future. If every day we fuel solely for the future, we could easily fall foul of an accumulative energy deficit.

Could - Send the consistent information to your body including insulin and other hormone control and taste

No point taking food you don't enjoy the taste of. Eating will become a focal point of your day. You will sit around your tent joking and ribbing each other so take foods that you like the taste of. A higher fat and protein content of your food will help control your satiety, blood sugar, emotional state and will also help to avoid irrational decisions during fatigue.

Would - Avoid any potential for constipation, sickness and or diarrhoea

Sounds obvious, but constipation, sickness and diarrhoea are to be avoided in the desert. Each is unpleasant in its own way and will add more pressure to your personal administration, enjoyment of the event and obviously, your performance.

When to eat is just as important as what

Each day I would follow a couple of simple guidelines with regards to snacks and refuelling.

I would aim to start the day fully hydrated with all my bottles filled with fresh water. I would have my day's snacks to hand made up of pork scratchings, nuts and other high-fat, portable food. This would stave off hunger and help take my mind off the terrain for a few minutes as and maintain a constantly supply of fat to my digestive system. Many people wait until they feel the symptoms of thirst and hunger before they begin their mid-race nutrition, but I would start 40 mins in religiously and maintain regular small snacks every 40 mins. I believe it is far better to control energy levels than allow them to peak and trough freely.

In addition, one 750ml drinks bottle containing a weak sports electrolyte drink that I wore on my hip. I would use this practically, to wash down some of the drier snacks and nutritionally to top up blood and liver sugar levels.

Along with a couple of pieces of chewing gum, I had a packet of jelly like high-sugar sports snacks to snack on. This is your nitrous oxide. I would eat a couple of chunks prior to sudden or powerful bursts of intense activity or anything which requires the use of the anaerobic energy systems such as large climbs or tough terrain.

The chewing gum was used on long flats only and would not only give me a small blood sugar spike due to lots of sugar receptors in the mouth, but the chewing would act as a metronome and set a rhythm for my jogging or marching pace.

You can see images and details of all the food I took at RunningLightBook.com/resources

In this chapter, I outlined my strategy for food

during the event. I hope you consider the brief explanations I made and start to question the mass marketing idea of running on sugars. Maybe you will consider becoming a fat burner in the future or even test it for yourself. You can find more information at the accompanying website, but also during one of my Running Light Presentations. See dates and locations at RunningLightBook.com. In the next chapter, we will look at kit and equipment.

PART 4

CHAPTER 14

KIT
(ESTIMATED 10% OF YOUR MDS SUCCESS)

Another area where MDS runners really get themselves into a quibble is the kit, but there really is no need for it. In this chapter, I will explain how you are setting yourself up for a tough time in the desert by incessantly worrying about the weight of your pack. I will also share why shaving 100g here and going without the food and comforts is a bad idea for most us.

Before we get into the kit and weight, take a second to consider the guy who ran the MDS with an ironing board strapped to his back! When most people are cutting off elastic from our packs to give ourselves the very best chance of success, he completed the same distance, over the same terrain and appeared to be smiling a hell of a lot more than most runners so why?

He had the right mindset. In his preparation, he had created future memories of him running with an ironing board strapped to his back. He had pre-programmed his mind how his body should act when it finds itself in the desert with a 10kilo slab of steel hanging off him. We can use similar tricks.

In the Marines, it was the same, some guys just could not leave their kit alone. They would be up all night packing and repacking, stitching elastic to their packs to attach new items that were meant to make things easier for them.

For an average runner, a couple of 100 grams is not going to make the slightest bit of difference physically, but once again it's the mental game you are playing in. Here's the problem...

There're two main issues. The first being your mind's inability to process a negative. Think back to the sign 'Wet Paint Don't Touch'. Then we touch it! Our mind deletes the negative and we must think about the thing before we can think about not doing it.

If I say, 'Don't think about the front cover of this book'... see there you go. You must think about it to not think about it. Now you try. Here's a sentence, one that you may have played to yourself a few times over the last few months, read it, but delete the (underlined) negative words.

'I don't want to carry too much weight in the desert.'

'I don't want to struggle because I am carrying too much kit'

'The really don't want to burn vital energy because my kit is too heavy'

So really, you are just reinforcing the fact that you do WANT all the things above, but that's not the only issue. Every time we think about struggling with weight while trekking across the Sahara we must play the video clip in our minds. We must think about it by imagining ourselves struggling on some sandy dune in baking 50-degree heat. These images are played out in our limbic region of the brain and this little critter is literal. It does not know the difference between a proper memory or a future memory. By continuously imagining ourselves struggling with the weight of our packs we are creating a programme for our mind to follow when we finally get to the Sahara.

Your ego will want to prove itself right and let's face it, you are lining yourself up for a whole world of hurt and worry.

Weight is weight, right?

Today I was a little bamboozled when an expert running coach boasted that he had shaved over 400 grams from his client's backpack. I felt a little insulted as a human being when he suggested 'You have to know what you are doing'... I have been using scissors for quite a while now have never had any issues. Anyway... the post got a lot of interaction from others looking to shave grams. In my mind, and sorry for getting a little cross, I could shit more than that! Sorry, the Marine comes out every now and again, but seriously. In the winter before the MDS, I eradicated sugar from my diet and dropped 8 kilos in a month and a half.

The truth is unless you are an elite level runner the weight will have very little bearing. It's how you think about the weight that counts. Or in my case, how you refuse to think about the weight.

So what? Well, again we are getting into elite level hacks for average runners. If you want to complete the MDS 400 grams is going to make very marginal differences to you physically. Mentally it may well plague you to think that if you had shaved off the 400g you would be so much quicker over the sand. Let's ditch that idea right now.

There are certain items you HAVE to take. No need to labour over the selection of these. I just bought a ready pack of the compulsory items from MyRaceKit, kept them in a zip lock bag and kept them in my bag.

Compulsory items:

- Backpack MDS or equivalent
- Sleeping bag
- Head torch and a complete set of spare batteries
- 10 safety pins,
- Compass, with 1° or 2° precision

- Lighter
- Whistle
- Knife with metal blade
- Tropical disinfectant
- Anti-venom pump
- A signalling mirror
- One aluminium survival sheet
- One tube of sun cream
- 200 euro or equivalent in foreign currency
- Passport
- Original medical certificate provided by AOI completed in and signed by the doctor
- Original ECG and its tracing

Supplied by the event organisers:

Marathon kit issued during the technical and administrative checks in Morocco by the organisation and will include the following:

- A road-book
- A distress beacon
- A ChronoTag
- Salt tablets
- Bags for the toilets
- ID marks

- A luminous stick (issued at CP3 of the non-stop stage)

My personal selection of kit

In addition to the kit listed I took the following:

- Inflatable sleeping mat (small)
- Approx. 3ft of Duck-tape for emergency kit repairs
- Sun glasses
- Ear plugs
- Long handle titanium spoon
- Wemmi wipes
- 4 Pack - Soapopular Pens - Antibacterial Hand Sanitiser Spray
- Pits & bits
- Waterproof notebook
- Retractable pencil
- GoPro with rugged case & 3 spare batteries
- UV lip salve
- Large adhesive strapping tape
- Lightweight silk sleeping bag liner

Clothing:

- Lightweight desert long sleeve running shirt (Raidlight)

- Shorts (Lululemon)
- 3 x Pairs of Thorlo running socks
- Asics Gel-Fujirunnegade trainers
- Raidlight desert gaiters
- Desert running hat
- 2 x UV protective Buffs
- Lightweight down jacket
- Skins full length compression pants

In this chapter, I outlined the kit you must take along, and the kit I chose to take. You can see how I packed the kit and why at RunningLightBook.com/Resources. In the next chapter, I'll go much deeper into weight. By the end, you should be able to make decisions you are happy with regarding the kit and weight you choose.

CHAPTER 15

WEIGHT

In this section, I want to explore the topic of weight. It's something that people really obsess and beat themselves up about. I'll present my theory on weight shortly, but before we start I want you to know that there is no need to over think this.

In 2001, I deployed with the Royal Marines into the mountains of Afghanistan. It was expected that we would run into 1,000's of Taliban fighters holed up in CIA funded battle trenches and tunnels. We needed to go in heavy! Our packs would weigh more than 200lbs with the bulk of the weight being ammunition, communication gear, thermal imagery, mortar bombs and more. The amount of operational, mission critical gear left no room for bare necessities. Sleeping bags were left out in place of bags of saline for IV's, our daily calorie ration was halved in place of enhanced body armour for protection during the close quarter battle deep in the formidable tunnels and ramparts.

Many of the younger guys under my charge struggled at first. During preparations for the operation, they obsessed for days. Constantly packing, unpacking and repacking... you get the idea! I first realised we needed to stop this when I found myself getting more fatigued during what was supposed to be 'enforced rest'. Each day was packed with mission-specific activities. We studied the limited mapping and intelligence we had, conducted mission rehearsals, liaised with our US counterparts that would provide fast jet support - packing kit had to take a back seat. That meant lots of the 'kit fiddlers' would mess around with their kit at night and lose vital sleep (disrupt my frikkin sleep!).

It had to change! Tired and frustrated, I leapt up one night and shouted "it's fucking easy... pack anything critical to the mission, then add your non-negotiables. After that, if there is doubt in your mind that you may be ok without it... leave it out. Then sort out anything 'nice-to-have-hand' then get your head down!" Eventually, they got it and we all got some sleep and I beat myself up for kicking off for a while. The guys were just trying to make the best choice they could. They had all the best intentions, but little experience of what they did need to take. I guess they just needed some guidance... like you.

So, here's my 4-step process for keeping

weight to a minimum and selecting the right kit for you. Here's basically how it flows:

#1 - Mission critical

#2 - Non-negotiables

#3 - If there is doubt there is no doubt (and it's out!)

#4 - Nice-to-have-to-hand

Start by ditching the right weight.

Let's not fluff around this. No point shaving a few grams from your pack when you're carrying a few kilos around your waist!

During my preparation, I vividly remember seeing a post in the Facebook group about reducing pack weight. Somebody was like, "Oh yeah. I've just stripped 400g off my bag and if anyone wants to know how to do it, then I'll gladly show you...".

At the time, I thought... "400g no shit... well I'll see your 400g's and raise you to 8,000g's!!! Beat that!"

Yep, you read that right. I shaved 8kg of excess weight prior to the race. How... The Christmas before I completely cut out sugar from New Year's Eve onwards. Within about 6 weeks, I'd lost 8 kilos. I'm not a huge bloke. I don't carry a lot of excess weight but to lose 8 kilos in just a few weeks is phenomenal and far greater than spending hours obsessing about cutting and slicing straps in half to save weight. Think about Pareto's rule (aka 80/20 rule - in that 80% of your results will come from 5% of your actions) and what's going to give you the best bang for your buck. Reducing body weight has a far greater advantage to your performance as you will run lighter, be more mobile, have a better strength relative to your muscle mass, consume less energy over each mile and your arse won't look like two squirrels fighting over a nut in a bin bag as you run along in your lycra.

It doesn't have to be tough either. Just cut out sugar. Whenever you look at foods to eat, if there is sugar in the top 5 ingredients, don't eat it. Some of the big things that you can swap out to make a huge difference are refined table sugar, alcohol, fruit and white carbohydrates, like potatoes, bananas, pasta, rice and bread.

Swap in green, leafy veg and good natural fats like coconut oil, avocado, some nuts and seeds and you can rapidly drop a few kilos in a couple of weeks which is far greater than 400 grams off your bag. Ok... you are going to have to work at it especially if you eat a predominantly carb heavy diet right now but how your physical ability will increase because your body weight is lighter.

Get your kit bag in order

Now let me clear something up, I cut unwanted straps and fittings from my MDS bag and I ditched pouches and evaluated kit to avoid taking too much, but I certainly didn't obsess about it. That's the difference. I think the heaviest bag this year was about 16.4kg and the lightest was 6.5kg.

The problem was having a light bag does not guarantee you a great finish time and having a heavy bag doesn't mean you will not finish!

A light bag means you will go without some nice-to-have's maybe cold at night and will have restricted meals and water... can you cope with that? If yes, go for it.

A heavier bag will mean you will have more food, more comforts, may sleep, eat and drink better... would you rather that?

I read stories of people packing, unpacking and re-packing over and over and heard about people waking in the night to check they have their spoon packed. I hate to hear of anyone losing sleep and worrying about anything so here's my advice.

I found that I was cutting straps off because I didn't want them dangling around and I just wanted my bag to be as simple as I could. I aim for tidy because tidy usually means well packed. The official MDS bag is a little over-engineered so I cut a few things off because they were flapping all over the place or had no noticeable use.

There's a saying in the Marines, pack early and you pack twice. All you're doing is agitating your mind really and you're just winding yourself up. Get it packed. That will do. You're going to repack it on the way anyway. Everybody did. You have a day to do administration before the race starts. You have nothing else to do other than sort your kit and hand your bags in and get processed.

If you want an activity to obsess over get the

sauna or start stretching. Maybe a bit of meditation or some affirmations. There's just better stuff you can be doing your time than fiddling with your bag.

Parkinson's law

Also, consider reducing the amount of space that you have in your bag. If you take a big bag, you're going to fill a big bag and if you take a small bag, you're going to fill a small bag. Having a small bag will cause you to be critical of what you take.

This is like Parkinson's law which roughly states 'a project will expand to fill the amount of time you give it'. It's the same with your kit for the MDS. Your kit will expand or shrink to fit the space that you give it so minimise space which, by its nature, will help you keep the weight down. As an example of this, I avoided the large front pouch on the MDS bag. I refused to allow myself the capacity to take an extra 2 or 3 kilos.

#1 - Mission critical

Now if you don't have the compulsory items, you're not actually doing the race so it's got to be in there. When packing the compulsory, mission critical kit I considered two things. I knew it was unlikely that I would use it so I just had it wrapped up and protected from sweat and the elements in little zip locked bags. Then I packed it away so that it was ready to hand if we got a kit inspection. I don't have to go dragging all the kit out just for the kit inspection. I had done that in the Marines far too often. I would pack compulsory, but rarely used items at the bottom of began and the instructors would always ask to inspect them. I would then have to drag all my dry, well-packed kit out into the mud.

#2 - Non-negotiables

The next thing is your non-negotiables. These are personal to you so be responsible for your decision. For example, I was quite happy going without an mp3 player, conversely, lots of other runners wanted music. Some people wanted a certain amount of comfort at night. I thought I'd get away with it and do all right and still be able to function so I made and owned that decision. Work out what your non-negotiables are. Write them down.

#3 - If there is doubt there is no doubt (and it's out!)

If after reading this, you are still hell bent on keeping weight to a minimum then apply the third rule. If you pick up a piece of kit and in your mind, you think "Do I really need this?" then that doubt suggests there is no doubt. Ditch it or at least put it in your hold baggage for the flight.

Have the peace of mind that nothing on the 'doubt' list is irreplaceable. It can either be replaced by someone else or an alternative improvised. Let's take a spare spoon for example. Your main spoon breaks and you no longer have a spoon. Ask your tent mates if they have a spare, borrow your buddies (just maintain good standards of hygiene) or cut up a plastic water bottle make one. Failing that you can make all your food a little wetter than you intended and drink it!

Your mind is an amazing thing and desperate situations trigger improvisation even in the least practical person. If you are considering a spare spoon, spare this and spare that... then you will do well to trust your mind more than you currently are.

#4 - Nice-to-have-to-hand

Finally, spare a moment for the things that you will need to hand. Examples being sun cream, alcohol gel, paracetamol, salt tablets, sunglasses etc. There was a guy that I met on the plane flying out called Liam. He was phenomenal. He was close to me throughout the event, though, as many were, he was much fitter than me. I kept overtaking him then he would overtake me and I would overtake him again. Each time I passed him he would have a trainer off or his bag open. He would be fiddling with a water bottle or rooting in his backpack for something. It was this basic administration and kit packing that slowed him down and really stopped him from just motoring and doing better than he did.

For me, some of the obvious ones, sun cream,

you never want to go rooting to put sun cream on. Your salt tablets, your race day snacks, water bottles need to be at hand so you can drink them. I also kept my recovery shake to hand for two reasons. First, if I was really struggling that day, then I knew I had something extra to hand but also, I started my recovery a couple of kilometres from the finish line. I would get my recovery shake out, I'd mix it with the water, and then I'd be sipping that as I was walking in.

Other stuff, hand sanitizer, I kept that at hand in case I'd go to the toilet and wanted that. Your water card, make sure that's easy to get your hands on so you can save time at the checkpoint. The final one was a Go-Pro. I had the Go-Pro to hand so I can just whip that out. I didn't have to mess around too much when I was catching those videos and pictures.

Everything else. I just packed it in a manner that was comfortable and distributed the weight well.

I made some sacrifices. Went without a couple of things but then again it was my choice and I owned the choice. Just like you must. Whatever choice you make, just know that you've made that choice in a rational state. Don't allow irrational mindset to beat you up about it.

In this chapter, I explained a 4-step system for assessing, selecting and packing the kit you take. Again, you can see how and where I packed the items I took at RunningLightBook.com/Resources. In the next few chapters I want to explain a couple of other important points before you go.

PART 5

CHAPTER 16

BEFORE
YOU GO

Writing this book has been every bit of a challenge, just like the MDS. I didn't wake one morning with 55,000 words in a word document. This is my third book so in that respect, I have written more books than I have done multi-stage ultra's but that doesn't take away the fears and worries when you release a book. Like the MDS, once you get going you are laid bare... staked out in the sun and free from criticism. I must say I haven't really thought about that. 'I'll deal with that later!' I thought.

It's been a long process (9 months) compared to the three months I expected. I imagined banging the first edition out within 12 weeks of the race ending, but as we discovered earlier, that would have been ideal... but the 'ideal' doesn't exist. Life gets in the way. At times, all I could do was write what I could when I could. One sentence at a time, sometimes one word at a time knowing that every word is a step closer towards my goal. Those words didn't always come easy and at other times whole paragraphs would spew onto the page. In fact, like training for the MDS, I had to get my wife to come and rescue me a few times!

So, before we end this journey together I want to introduce a couple of people that helped me along the way. Each has inspired me and helped sculpt my mindset, taught me valuable lessons and well... basically been a fucking good egg!

I recorded short interviews with them first and foremost because I respect what they say, but also because it's an easy few thousand words for the book. Seriously, though, before we part I want to thank you for your attention. Did you know that humans simply cannot feel anger or frustration when they are grateful? Gratefulness is a tool that my wife Paula promotes every day as a method to dispel a negative mindset and help people out of a rut. If you still feel stuck with your training or with life in general, look at your surroundings and list the things you are grateful for. Even the smallest thing can help negative shit fade to nothing.

I am incredibly grateful for you taking the time to read this book. I am even more grateful that you are seizing the opportunity to challenge yourself. As humans, we need exciting futures to pull us through life not exciting pasts that keep pulling us back to relive the same shitty cycles as guilt, a lack of congruence, anger, frustration and a lack of self-worth! Back in the 'Eorl' days, I was full of those things and to sit here now in completely different surroundings with an exceptionally exciting future ahead of me.

I was done! I had pretty much tapped out of life, but deep down I harboured a tiny seed of desire. A desire to regain life and to become more than a homeless vet with fucked up memories and a chequered past. The seed started to grow when Eorl the wanker dog from hell got me off my arse. The truth is we cannot possibly change when we are sat stagnant. We cannot steer a parked car, right? If we stay in one position, we lock in our current state within the body. If we move we allow our state to change. Running with Eorl became the first few scrapes of soil where the tiny seed began to sprout. I consider the following people to be nutrient rich water that helped the seedling grow. Paula is the gardener who checks my leaves, rights my stem and cuts back the shit when necessary, but you guys... watching you guys prepare and conquer challenges is the sunlight! I hope the following interviews inspire you and guide you. I hope the pages before now have given you hope, a deep-rooted desire and belief in yourself as the apex predators you are. I hope you have a few giggles along the way and I hope you have struggled to accept some of the things I have written. Ultimately, if our thoughts and beliefs control everything we do, the best thing I can do is challenge your thinking.

To you and your tent mates, even if you don't know them yet... good luck and safe journey. Please accept one huge fist pump from me and please, if this book has helped in any way... even if you burnt the first 30 pages to heat your noodles in the desert let me know by visiting RunningLightBook.com/resources

You can also ask me questions, see where I will be delivering the Running Light presentations and training days and generally banter me on Facebook at www.facebook.com/groups/RunningLight/

CHAPTER 17

FROM THE
EXPERTS & PAST RUNNERS

Interview With Phil Quirk
Performance Coach To Athletes, High Level
Excutives And Entreprenuers

Phil Quirk is one part of an amazing dynamic duo that I first met while working on a TV documentary. The documentary is yet to be aired, but consisted of a series of challenging selection weekends for an expedition to retrace Shackleton's route over the South Pole.

Before we start...

Both Phil Quirk and his business partner Phil Kelly (featured elsewhere in this book) became great friends, mentors and influences in my life. Motivational speaker Jim Rohn famously said that

'We are the average of the five people we spend the most time with'. I would gladly spend every working minute with these two... though I am sure their partners would have something to say.

The start...

PQ and I sat in my garden with a glass of water, the sun was beating down and it was a beautiful day. It was always a privilege to get time with either Phil as their business is growing so rapidly they are constantly on the move.

Having coached professional rugby players, footballers, golfer (never really understood them!) ... Para-Olympians and Olympians alike, I was looking for an exclusive insight into how Phil motivates them and maximises their potential using only the top 6" of their bodies.

I asked him how he is coaching athletes for the Rio games, but fundamentally how we as non-Olympians or full-time athletes can use the tricks and techniques to prepare for the Marathon Des Sables.

After a few minutes of shit blokey banter where I crucified his dress sense, we got down to the nitty-gritty.

Me - Phil, thank you for joining me today...

Phil interrupts - It's ok I had nowhere else to stay...!

Me - ...I asked you here today to discuss the Marathon Des Sables as I know, from my own experience and what has been written on the MDS FB group that there are hundreds of people every year that struggle to prepare for the race.

Can you share with us a couple of simple strategies that have proven to be big hitters during your elite Athletes Program...?

Phil - No worries Craig, well I want to start by introducing a strategy that we developed and use every day now, that was first introduced in 'Seven Habits of Highly Effective People', the bestselling book by Stephen Covey.

Covey describes two metaphorical circles in every person's life. One called the circle of influence and the other the circle of concern. Now every factor in your life belongs to one or the other circle. They cannot straddle circles and there is a definite demarcation between the two.

Starting with the circle of concern. Within the circle of concern are all the factors in your life, training and preparation that are affecting athletes right now, but which they can do nothing about! They are the things keeping them awake at night and that they are worrying about and obsess over. Now these worries and woe's feel very real and have a huge smothering effect on anyone caught in that circle, but there's little to nothing you can do about them.

Craig - MDS examples being the heat, we cannot change how hot it will be during the or how cool it will be at night?

Phil - Exactly... or the terrain. You cannot change it and you won't even know the route until you get your road book... we simply cannot do anything about it.

So, let's head back in time to our prehistoric brain... which I know you can relate to Craig!

Craig - Showing off Phil... I'll just leave it out of the book!

Phil - Our brain developed the propensity to look for danger and look for negatives. It kept us alive. We are pretty mediocre animals with nothing in the way of armour or weaponry. We don't have a huge beak, talons, sharp teeth, the speed of a cheetah or the venom of a snake. We used our brains to protect ourselves with 'fight or flight'.

Which is actually wrong... it's not fighting or flight, we freeze as many of the predators of the time had poor eyesight, run and hide and then when cornered will fight. But the fight is a last resort.

Craig - So we are pre-programmed to look for the negatives...?

Phil - Exactly... and to be over cautious! It kept us alive and today, as we have few predators, focusing on what might happen stops us looking like a dick, appearing stupid or embarrassing ourselves and failing. But playing it cautious never got anybody anywhere. We would never have broken the 4-minute mile if Roger Bannister hadn't committed to doing so, we wouldn't have mastered manned flight or crossed the huge oceans.

Craig - The 'freeze' part really strikes me. I think that's where so many people are right now. overwhelmed and struggling to 'unfreeze'.

Thinking about it I can see the next stage 'flight (run & hide)' too. People 'running away and doing other things, hiding from what needs to be done.

Phil - Exactly... Operating in the circle of concern is frustrating, demotivating, steals your energy and is often very destructive. It will root you to the ground and stop progress and training dead in its tracks. Our powerful yet primitive brains smother our rational modern day brain but you know what... we can quite easily change that.

Working in the circle of concern will stifle any progress that you try and make. You're not going to affect that kind of stuff. You're never going to get anywhere because you truly, no matter what action you take, cannot do anything about it.

It's a bit like trying to take on 'what ifs'. What ifs haven't happened yet and you can't really affect anything that either has happened in the past or has not happened in the future. You can only use the present.

There's a great book called 'Why Zebras Don't Get Ulcers' by Stanford biologist Robert Sapolsky. The author explains that zebras don't stress over 'What if's...' If they did they would be fat, get ill all the time, have disrupted sleep, pick up injuries and have ulcers and heart problems through stress. Some of those symptoms will be familiar to some people, but the point is zebra's only deal with the 'now'. You can only change the present right now. That means working within the circle of influence.

Craig - You're right Phil... I have never ever seen a zebra in a doctors waiting room.

Phil - Let's look at the circle of influence. The main factor for any idiot who volunteers to run 250km in 6 days through the Sahara Desert is your own mindset. Just looking at how you can step out of the rut, how you can lay the foundations to a series of small wins, a history of success, as opposed to a history of struggle and failure and not really getting anywhere. You can affect how you prepare by working towards being just a fraction better today than you was yesterday.

The day you arrive for the Marathon Des Sables, you can and will only do the best you can and that's pretty much what it's about. It's not about comparing yourself to other people unless you're an elite runner. It's about getting through and having the best experience you can. Craig, you proved that you are much more likely to excel when you remove self-imposed pressures.

Otherwise, you're going to be one of those runners that went out there measuring themselves against the elite runners, failed or dropped short and now feel they've got unfinished business in the desert.

Craig - Personally, I was 100% confident that what I wanted was the experience, my position was secondary. I ended up exceeding my expectations on both counts. It was on unforgettable experience and I placed much higher than I expected.

Phil - For the ultimate preparation for any

athlete taking part in arduous events or very competitive races, I encourage everyone to remain in their circle of influence.

Craig - And is there an easy way to check where you are Phil?

Phil - Draw it out... commit it to paper. Draw the two circles and consider all the factors right now and place them in the circle. Ask a friend to help you or share it on the Running Light FB Page. Then check in every time you feel demotivated.

Other things would be your kit, making sure the kit is right for you, not the same as anybody else's. It doesn't need to be the same. It just needs to be right for you. Same with your food, same with your water strategy. Just work on something that works for you, not based on anyone else.

Be careful who you take advice from because they maybe a different level to you, they have more experience than you, they have a different race strategy. Perhaps they don't even have a strategy at all, so be very careful about comparing yourself or making decisions based on other people's stuff. It's got to be your decision because you've got to be content with it during the event.

Another factor is how you handle things change. Things will change. Life is going to get in the way. It's going to throw all sorts of different stuff at you and it's going to distract you from your program, from your plan.

Craig - In the military, there's a saying that 'no plan survives contact with the enemy'. Basically, the minute you encounter the enemy, then your perfect plan is going to go wrong. Factors from the circle of concern that you cannot do anything about will start to cause an effect. How do you deal with that?

Phil - Change Craig... nothing goes wrong, the circumstances just change. 'Wrong' initiates freeze, flight & fight'. 'Change' initiates a desire to look for options and other courses of action. 'Wrong' is static and doesn't suggest progression. 'Change' is transient and suggests movement. If lost in the desert I would rather have movement in my head.

Craig - Love it

Phil - Stay within the circle of influence. When things change, think about it, okay, is it in the past? I can do nothing about the past. I cannot change the past. All I can do is shape the future using the present right now.

Craig - Elsewhere in the book I have explained the use of past, present and future as tools. Basically, the three time periods in your life, the past, the present, and the future, are just tools to be used like you would use a hammer or screwdriver. Focus your energy on using those tools in the right way, you would not use a hammer to fix a screw or a screwdriver to drive a nail. Use the future to excite you. Think about the race, the finish and your reception back home. Think about everything that you know about the race and then the reasons why you want to complete it and use that to create a deep-rooted desire within you. Use the past to give you confidence. What have you done in the past to prove that you can get through this?

Of course, it may not be on the same level but look for similarities. It could just be, well I'm an experienced runner. I'm well above average in my club, I've been running now for a couple of years, a couple of months, or whatever. It could be that you know you can operate in these temperatures because I've done it before or your knowledge leads you to believe that humans have occupied every continent of the world and are incredible at managing heat and cold.

Phil - Yep... or... 'I know that I've got the right mindset to get through this because I've tested myself in the past. This maybe a little unnerving, BUT I know I can rise to the level once I'm there and I'm caught up in that environment.'

Use the past to create confidence and then use the present to start building momentum. Use it as the tool that it is. It's a way for you to generate an unstoppable force. That's done by tiny steps each day. Everyday striving for just a little bit more. Think... 'today I just want to get that little bit better than I was yesterday!'

It doesn't matter how good we get, how far we go, how much faster we are. It just matters that we did something a little bit better than we did yesterday.

That can be in so many ways, not just our running ability. It can be the fact that you ran for a couple of minutes longer today. It could be that you ran a little bit faster. Maybe you carried a little bit more weight? It could be that you went a slightly different route, or it just means that you were more consistent or whatever.

Aim to be that little bit better. That's all that needs to be and then... when the time comes, you'll be in a far better state to do this than if you piled all the pressure on and just stifled yourself, completely overwhelmed yourself, and not being able to get going.

Craig - Thanks, Phil. The two-circle theory is a keeper for everyone preparing for the race and I would say learning to 'check-in' when times get tough is more beneficial than any hill sprint or energy gel.

Phil - My pleasure Craig and good luck to all those that are heading out for the race.

It was an incredible chat with PQ who, like I said, has done some amazing work with motivating and maximising the thought processes of athletes and high-level executives as well as dragging my head out of a shitty hole at times.

If you want to learn more about Phil Quirk & Phil Kelly, then you can find him on Facebook, HBP-NLP or HBP Training. They're two slightly different angles to this business, or you can go to his website, hbp-nlp.com.

CHAPTER 18

INTERVIEW WITH
TONY SHERIDAN

**Marathon Des Sables, Atlantic Rower
& Everest Base Camp**

The following chapter is a transcription from a man who helped me during my preparation. He was the first to highlight the fact that much of the MDS is run in your head. We met through Julie, a friend and client that I had coached at TEAM Bootcamp. I often spoke about my goal of completing the MDS to create accountability, a public declaration is much harder to back out of than promises we make to ourselves. Julie mentioned she knew someone that had done it the previous year. Like everyone involved in the race, I had a thirst for knowledge and top tips, but we never really engaged until the day I posted a video in the FB group. I filmed the video on what seemed to be a perfect summer evening for running. The sun was low and setting in the sky creating an amazing sunset. At the time, I was suspected much of what was being posted in the FB group was bollocks and bravado. I knew that most people posting were either full of shit or kidding themselves and there were many more people nervous to post their incredibly low on motivation. I posted the video publically to see if others spoke out. The result of that video was my first real insight into the brotherhood and camaraderie surrounding the MDS. I received hundreds of messages from past and future runners and support staff, but I also received many messages from others feeling low in motivation. I posted the video about 9 months from the start and I knew it was perfectly normal to lack motivation at that point. The oldest and often most powerful part of the brain has two main directives. Number 1 is scan for danger… it can scan our surroundings and assess hundreds of bytes of data up to 5 times a second. incredible eh? But it's the second directive that effects our motivation… Primitive Brain directive number 2 is to seek rest. The brain is a responsible for a huge number of calories consumed and it will seek to limit the number of calories it burns through to prolong survival. Our brain basically starts to switch off. The event is so far ahead in time that it fails to register in our primitive brain. Anyway… out of all the messages I received Tony's stood out.

The essence of his message is captured during this interview following the 2016 MDS. Tony was also one of the major stories from the 2014 event after suffering horrendous blisters that make even the most severe injuries seem trivial. Tony would feature in Runners World as he peeled his feet from blood soaked socks at the end of each day and limped over each dune refusing to give in.

Craig - Hey Tony.

Tony - Hello mate, how are you?

Craig - Yeah, I'm great. Thanks for joining me on this little chat about the MDS and your experiences. You've been out there twice now. Which probably makes you one of the most experienced people in the MDS? I would say because I don't think a lot of people do it more than once…

Tony - A couple of die-hards do, mate, but few have my experience. I've experienced both ends of the spectrum now with my DNF this year, but also getting through with my feet as bad as they were two years ago.

Craig - So a bit of background… I owe a big part of my finishes medal to you really because we had lots of chats before we went out there and I took so much from the things you said. I thought it would be great to share some of your advice and experience in this book. Before we get into that, can you tell us how you first came to know about the MDS and where you go the crazy idea from?

Tony - Right. 2011, I was sat in Starbucks reading Men Only magazine. At the time, I was training for my first half marathon, The Great North Run. I was looking for top tips and I came across an article about the MDS. I read about the people doing it and something clicked and I thought, "I'll do that!" I found an email address, emailed them and they said, "Next year is full and the year after is full. Next February we'll start sending out information about getting a place." I hadn't heard anything by March, I emailed them, they said, "We have a problem with the website." I refused to let it lie.

I emailed them again in April... still having problems. Then I got an email in May saying, I remember it now "12th of June, 10AM applications go live." The organisers explained that the places would get snapped up within minutes and that I would receive a form... have the answers already typed out and then copy and paste them into the form to submit it as quickly as possible. This point was the first time I had to come clean to my family. I had kept secret until now, but I was so shit on a computer I had to tell my daughter so she could do the cutting and pasting for me. Her comment then was the first time I heard what was to become a very common statement to me... "You're mad, you'll die!"

I submitted the form and received "Congratulations on your confirmed place." I just thought it was a generic email. Then it asked me for my blood group and passport number! I started thinking, "Shit, I've really signed up... I might actually really die!" You could also join the Facebook group and as you know the Facebook group is a big part of it. I decided to join the Facebook group and that was it! I was to run the MDS, though it hadn't really sunk in yet.

The next morning, I was accepted into the Facebook group. I was the first person in, no surprise there, and I was the first person to post something and I said, "Because I'm in the group am I on the MDS?" The comments started coming in. Someone else posted, "Yeah, am I in?" About 6 or 7 of us all asking the same question. Then someone posted a link with the names of the confirmed places. Of course, with my second name being Sheridan it was way down the list, I quickly scrolled all the way down until I got to R and then I started slowly single clicking down. Next thing… there is my name and I just thought, 'oh!'

Craig - You've done it?! Lol… I personally love the reaction you get from most people when they hear you have completed the MDS. It was a huge draw to me.

Tony - Right. I put on Facebook, 'I'm in the MDS!' My daughter Amber replied, 'You idiot!' That summed it up really and that was it, I had 22 months to prepare.

Craig – So, on to your preparation for your first MDS. Did it all go to plan?

Tony – Well I think everyone thinks they could have prepared better than they did. Life gets in the way but I was fit… There was a lot of people doubting me but I knew in my head that I'd crack it. In fact, other people's doubt is probably the thing that made me succeed that time.

Craig - Yeah... Just proving the doubters wrong. So... during your first MDS, you rapidly became a big story of interest and would eventually feature in Runners World because of the state of your feet. What's the story? ...and just for this interview, readers should know that this wasn't a result of bead foot care or failing to prepare. The soles of your trainers collapsed in the heat.

Tony – I had been told that a French lady a year before had to have reconstructive surgery on the soles of her feet. Anyway, I experienced just how destructive 270k of rolling sand dunes and jebels can be on your feet. During my preparation, a couple of mates who knew that I can be stubborn and head strong. I'll literally push and push myself and not give up. They took me aside and said, "Look Tony, if you get to a point where you're going to hurt and injure yourself, please do the right thing and stop!"

Well it's not always easy to do that sometimes, is it? The insole of my trainers rapidly deteriorated in the heat and collapsed from about 50mm to about 40mm. The Doc Trotters tried to fashion a new insole for me, but it didn't really help. It was like walking on a slope. My feet slipped and moved around in my trainers as I overcompensated for no support. I was walking totally out of kilter. I managed to struggle through most days on painkillers and by strapping my feet as best as I could. It took me a while to get going each morning, but the body soon turned off most of the pain making it 'almost' bearable.

The worst point was half way through the long day... I had stopped to check my feet at a check point. As I got back to the tent later than most each night, they hadn't really seen the state my feet were in. I couldn't get my feet back into my shoes. I was trying to slide them in and the fluid and blood was leaking out through the dressings, through my socks. My mate, Mark turned around and said, "Tony, I didn't realize your feet were that bad!" At that point, I took the dressings off and I remember 2 of the MDS crew had to carry me to the doctor. The doctor had the arse with me because she had been woken up. This was 6 in the morning so she had been out there all day, lol. She shouted at me! "Why have you stripped the dressings off your feet? Why have you done this?" I shouted back in pain, "Because they were soaking, they were green, they were red, they were soaking wet." Then she said, "I've got no more medicine!"

At that stage Craig, I wanted her to pull me out of the race. That was easier than quitting. I wanted her to say, you're out. If she said I'm out, brilliant, I could drop my guard, it wouldn't be my doing. Well... she didn't *laughs*! She patched my feet up. Then a funny thing happened... it just shows the power of the mind. You know what it's like out there Craig. People think that by stepping in other people's foot prints you won't sink... it's bollocks. You still sink... the best-case scenario is to find fresh sand that no one had broken the surface of. At night, it was terrible for me cos I couldn't see the footprints of others or the fresh sand and each time I stepped in a foot print or on uneven ground, the movement was exaggerated... so was the pain.

Then, it was ... We've been taking the piss within our tent about silly sayings. One of them was, 'it's always darkest before dawn' but long behold when this doctor was telling me off, I noticed it was light. I thought actually, I can pick my way through fresh sand now. I can reduce the pain and move quicker! I was spurred on by this. I got my shit together and somehow cracked on. I didn't slow. I think the last 4 miles took me 2 hours jacked up on Tramadol. "Can I have Tramadol?" I asked the doctor. "Have you had any?" She said, I told her know, but I had had 6 that day. I was convinced that the big jebel that day was on a turn table as I approached it, it seemed to move further away. You know yourself, that place gets to you!

At the end of the long day... and I don't do emotion mate. At the end of the long day, Steve Diederich, an absolute gentleman, came up to me as I crossed the finish line. He put his arms out and said, "Tony, yours has been one of the epic journeys this year. We can see you from half a mile away because of how you're limping." He said, "Go put your feet up and get a recovery drink." Tears immediately bubbled up and I walked away. Then, although I was one of the last in, all my tent was waiting there. I'd only met Andy Miller, 5 days before and there he was waiting with tears in his eyes. We shared a 'moment', but from that point on… I knew I would get my medal the next day.

Afterwards, I discovered the inner grey foam used in my trainers couldn't resist the heat. It happened to other people too, though it seems some of the women got around in them fine. Obviously, it was a combination of the crap foam and the weight of me that made the difference.

Craig – An amazing feat of determination Tony. A couple of questions then, did you class yourself as a runner before you decided you were going to do the MDS?

Tony - No, I classed myself as a bit of a pack horse.

Craig - Were you running regularly or was it ...

Tony - Yeah, well I was going out regularly though I hadn't really run much before I signed up. I was running on my own and sometimes doing up to half marathons. I plugged my headphones in and got out the door. I was doing fasted runs, up to 18 miles with a pack on towards the end, but not just running. I was doing a lot of leg strength work at the gym too. I cannot stress how important that is.

I could've done more. The one thing I'll say to anybody about the MDS, unless you're an elite runner, if you're someone who's running marathons, week in and week out, you'll run a lot of it, but you won't run it all. If you're someone like me, on the fringe of being a runner, you'll walk a lot more of it than you think. I think you found out yourself, didn't you?

Craig - Yeah, I quickly made up my mind that I wasn't going to even try running on the up hills and soft sand. I just didn't have the energy in my legs to do it. It just took so much out of me, but ... Yeah, let's crack on a little. We'll talk about the little things. I'll give you a topic and you give your spin on it. What's your one bit of advice for anybody looking to do the MDS? Let's say they fall into the same bracket as you and me. Those that just want to go out and have the experience and carry away that medal.

Tony - The thing that I recommend is that so many people think about so much about running with a pack on. They go out too soon. Even, Danny Kendall phenomenal athlete. A legend in the MDS, leaves his pack training until later. He said, "You don't need to be running 6 miles with a pack on, mate. You can build that up in 12 weeks. You can build that up in the new year."

Craig - Yeah, I agree with that. I know you can take anybody, shake them out. Get a little bit of stretching done with a bit of running under their belt. Crack a little consistent running and drop a bit of bodyweight and they can go crack it. I really do believe that.

Tony - Yeah, it's important to build up slowly.

Craig - What about kit, Tony? What were your big tips...? If you could pick out 3 big tips. 3 big hitting tips for kit, what would they be?

Tony - As light as possible, that's the big one. As light as possible and secondly, you must test it.

Craig - That's the tip that I heard most often. People still go out there without testing their kit.

Tony - I went out maybe 12 kilos in 2014 and it was too heavy. My kit weighed 6.9 this year.

Craig - Yeah, big difference and shows that so much of what you think is necessary is not needed.

Tony – Lastly... Food, test your food. I threw a load of food away 2 years ago. I knew my fitness wasn't where it should be this year and my body weight certainly wasn't... I was nowhere near as light as I was 2 years ago. I knew I needed to get my pack weight down to give myself half a chance.

Craig - Why do you think people go out there too heavy? Is it because they haven't tested it to work out what they can and cannot do without or is it because they want more comfort than they really need.

Tony - Yeah, that's it. You've hit the nail on the head. They think they need more than they really need... Little things soon add up camera, charger, GPS, extra food.

Craig - All right, cool. Moving on then. What about motivation, Tony? Particularly motivation in your training. Imagine people reading this book now. They have not done the MDS, yet. It's cold, it's wet, it's miserable in the UK winter. They try to motivate themselves to get out there. How was it for you? Did you have stacks of motivation or ...

Tony - I trekked up to Everest's Base Camp in 2012. One of the lads I was to do it with had to pull out as one of his kids was in one of the children's hospital in London and was very, very ill. She had pulmonary hypertension. The aorta, instead of expanding when you've got increased blood flow, it contracts. It's very, very rare ... It's a very serious illness I decided that I was going to do the MDS to raise money for her. I had a very personal and great cause for doing it. When I was out in the cold at night, you think to yourself, "You know what? I'm out here for 10, 12 miles. It's nothing really compared to what some of the people are going through." Then, of course the public accountability, the paper, people behind me. That all gets you motivated, doesn't it? That was the key to my motivation. The hardest thing isn't the running. It's stepping out of your doorstep.

Craig - It's getting out there, isn't it? In this book, I talk about making your 'Why' huge so the 'How' doesn't matter.

Tony - Yeah, you get in after work and think, "I'll go out in a minute after the news. Oh, it's too dark now." You know? That's one thing that I've always found. I prefer to go out in the evening.

Craig - I'm the same...

Tony – I can't get up at 5 to go for a run, I'd rather go out in the evening.

Craig – And that's a great tip for readers and one I stress to people all the time. If you know you prefer to run in the evenings, then don't force yourself to go running in the morning. There's enough stacked against you already.

Tony - It becomes a chore then, doesn't it?

Like my partner Sarah, she loves running in the morning. She says, "Let's go..." I make an excuse up. I'd rather come back from work. Get my stuff on, get my headphones and go out.

Craig - Yeah, okay. Next topic food... People obsess over a couple of things for the MDS. The kits one, food is another. What's your big-arsed tip regarding food?

Tony – It's very individual, but not an exact science really. You're talking 6 days. Taste and likes is less important than fuelling what you are doing and that includes recovery.

Craig - Would you agree that it's very unlikely you're going to get your food wrong?

Tony - Well you can get as deep into to it as you want and I know lots of people really obsess over it. This year we made and dehydrated our food ourselves. Then, we vacuum packed it so knew what was going into it.

Craig – For me I didn't take any of the expedition meals. I didn't like the taste when I tested them at the Expo. I just took some noodles with some chia seed, coconut oil and all that kind of stuff.

Tony - Pepperami's?

Craig - Yeah, Pepperami's, fantastic.

Tony - Yes, they were great. To be fair, I know that Sarah was looking at all the expedition meals. I decided I was going to take Supa-noodles and Pot Noodles along with porridge for breakfast.

Craig - I took Supa-noodles and they were brilliant with some chia seeds. I melted a little

Parmesan in there as well. In hindsight, I would've taken a couple of packs of porridge for the morning also.

Ok mindset stuff. First, how much do you think was in your head and how much was in your feet?

Tony - Your head will give in before your feet do. It's amazing what the human body can take. I didn't want to look at my feet, Craig. If I looked at my feet, it scared me. If I didn't look at my feet, I'd crack on. I'd feel another blister start. I could feel them build and build. Then, I go over some stones, some sharp pain. Every time my foot went down, I could feel a jet of water coming out of the blister, but the battle was in my head. I was constantly justifying why I should and shouldn't carry on. I was so close to jacking it all in.

Craig – I know how you feel I have been there. It can mess you up but do you agree it can also drive you on?

Tony - It did, it drove me on! I didn't want to look at my feet at all. The night before the long day I stripped all the dressings off and had a look. I wish I hadn't, my feet were in a terrible state. The trouble is, I knew that if I went to Doc Trotters that night I would wait for 2 hours to get seen. I'd then have to pick my way back to the tent in the dark and all my tent mates would be in their sleeping bags. I decided I would muddle some dressings together with my own first aid kit and then go going to Doc Trotters at the first checkpoint the next day.

Craig - That's a good idea, hard-core, but I get it!

Tony - Right? When I woke up that morning, I looked at the dressings, which were manky to say the least. It took me about an hour and 45 to get to the first checkpoint. I was there for 45 minutes and my mate was nearly sick as I had my feet treated. Even the doctor who dressed my feet, was grimacing.

Craig - What would you say to people that are starting to feel a little bit overwhelmed right now? Your story could be freaking them out a little. People say it's the toughest foot race on Earth and all that. Is it something that you should worry about? Is it something you've got to respect?

Tony - Yeah. I suppose Rory Coleman spoke about this, he came up to me just before this time. He poked my belly and said, "Oh my god, Tony. You have got fat!" Obviously, as you know, my preparation was nowhere near what it should've been this year. I had been unwell, I spent most of January in bed with shingles. Because of workload and recovering from a shoulder injury the year before, I couldn't do the training I wanted to. I thought I had 4 months after Christmas to create a plan and get out and crack it. Shingles fucked that up. In hindsight, maybe I should have deferred, but this year I was doing it with Sarah and wanted to be there as a couple. Rory (Coleman) said he has seen a lot of people on their second MDS fail to pay it the respect it deserves because it's their second time, they get complacent.

Craig - Really?

Tony - I think that's true. Complacency creeps in. I knew it was going to be tough. Yeah, I got complacent. I had done it once, and thought I could do it again. It can bite you and it did. It does need to be given respect, but a healthy respect. I think we have both proved that with some smart preparation and a tough mindset it's doable. For people feeling overwhelmed, you must prepare at your pace, in your own way and without comparing yourselves to others.

Craig - 100%. Earlier in the book I explain why many people get overwhelmed. They measure themselves against others. Even elite runners. If we looked at how the Moroccans are training and compared to how we were training. We would've been like, holy shit, how the hell are we going to go on. They win their race. You must run *your* race.

Tony - I'm a big fan of social media, but I do think sometimes it has its drawbacks. Comparing yourself to others and getting wound up being one of them. The other thing I do think is that when people say you can walk the MDS. Yeah, you can walk it, but it's a 'walk', not a walk! If you know what I mean.

Craig - Yeah, it's a faster walk. It's not a leisurely stroll on a Sunday afternoon kind of walk.

Tony – It's walking but with your head down and arms and legs pumping. You must crack on, mate.

Craig - I remember you saying to me that

people out there walking have a tougher race to an extent because there're out there longer. They need more water. Generally, they must carry more kit. They get less time to recover and must cook in the dark at night when the runners are in bed having got back much earlier.

Tony - Yeah, your feet are going to get hammered and you're exposed to the heat and sun much more. Less time rested. It's easy, though. Elizabeth (Barnes), believes that as well. She said she feels sorry for people who walk it because it's harder. Definitely is, definitely.

Craig - Okay, linked to overwhelm, what about self-induced pressure? People who just psych themselves out. Remember your Sarah posted in the Facebook one day saying, "Oh god, I'm looking at other people doing 20 miles a day and I'm barely doing 5k!" What would you say about that?

Tony - Once you get overwhelmed it can be hard to stop feeling overwhelmed, isn't it? It's... but people simply differ in training requirements. Take Sarah and I... I know that Sarah struggled with walking and long slow training, whereas I was struggling with the running. I banked on doing a lot more of walking this year which is why I emphasized walking during training. You know, if you haven't walked and have only run during training, it can be odd and exhausting when you get in the sand and you're forced to walk.

Craig - Different muscles working. Different energy systems too. Cool, so Tony, let's pretend that I've not been out there. I go into 'Tony, I'm shitting myself about this race." What would you say to me?

Tony – Take a minute and relax. Pick out some of the things going well for you instead of focussing on what's not going well and start to build on that. You must show respect, but with a few months training your body can do it, if you keep your head out of the way.

Craig - Massive part of getting excited about something is thinking about what's coming up. What are the real highlights to the MDS for you? What things stick out in your mind? What were the funny times, the celebratory times, the proud moments and all that?

Tony - Your tent mates make it, doesn't they? They play a huge part. It's the laugh you have when you're in your tents at night and in the mornings. When you're out in that course you're often on your own and you look forward to getting back to your tent. That's when you have a laugh. When you meet one of your tent mates out on the course too, at the checkpoints and water stops. I had some laughs in 14. It's the camaraderie, isn't it? Also, it's a beautiful part of the world.

Craig - I remember seeing every colour of sand you can imagine. It is an incredible part of the world. You're right.

Tony - Would you do it again?

Craig - I don't feel the need to do it again. I would if asked, but…

Tony - Exactly, that's the same as me. It's a

fantastic thing... to have an MDS medal and all the stories that go with it.

Craig - People hold it in high regard, even if you're modest about it yourself, you know what I mean?

Tony – Most people will say "I can't do it!" Well why not? I've done it, you can do it too. Ok, you will have to change a few things and train, but as we have discussed it is that mental approach. It starts with self-belief. From me reading that magazine, having never even run a half marathon. I thought, "Yeah, I'll do this!" It was a done deal.

Craig - Again I talk about that self-belief earlier in the book. The minute we start to question our ability it can be a slippery slide down. I used internal dialogue throughout the whole event. I would tell myself that it didn't have to be quick or pretty... it just had to be done!

How much of your self-belief was ignorance and not really knowing what you had let yourself in for?

Tony – Ha... probably quite a bit. I just thought to myself, "It can't be that hard."

Craig - Was it?

Tony - Yeah, it fucking was, but I got through... see, I knew it!

Did you ever see the video that I posted when I just left the last check point on the long day in 2014?

Craig - No.

Tony - Mate, I was doing a little bit of a video

diary selfie thingy. I was in bits and I said, 'I'll never do this again'. Then not long after I had signed up for it again! You forget the bad times!

Craig - They don't last forever, do they? The shit times pass, that's the thing.

Tony - The good memories stay with you. The camaraderie, just the laughs and stuff like that. Going into Dot Trotters and them calling their friends over cos your feet are that bad! Then, they get their phones out and take pics of your feet. Of course, getting your medal. I do remember a friend of mine, Brian Marsh, had to be pulled out. He jumped a rock and one of those big thorns went through his sole. He had to get someone with pliers to pull the thorn out of his foot. It was over for him. His feet were trashed. Unfortunately, now, I'd better go and get a best of 3, hadn't I?

Craig - Can we chat about that a little bit? We talk lots about doing it and being successful but what was it like when you realized that was it, you weren't going to make it this year?

Tony – This year was different. Day 1, was brutal with the terrain, wind and sand storms. I had a panic attack in the dunes. I thought I shit myself. I was vomiting. I couldn't see in the sand storm. The sand was that bad, we couldn't see where the checkpoint was. I ran out of water and I thought, "What the fuck am I doing back here, it's brutal!" I missed the cut off on the first day by 11 minutes. They said, "You're out." ...and I said, "Thank you!"

Craig - Seriously, is that what you said.

Tony – Yeah! And I fucking meant it! Then, they

came back to me, and said 'you may not be out.' Then, they come back and said I'm definitely out. 10 minutes later, they return and explain that I am not out, but have received a time penalty. I didn't have any food that night. I just got a recovery drink in. In my tent that night the sand was still whipping through the camp, wasn't it? After the first day, I just thought that's the hard day out of the way. On the long day, it's hard but because it's a long day, isn't it? I had to regain my thoughts to crack on after believing I was out. "Right, head down and crack on, 17 minute miles." I thought, "My packs going to get lighter, I'm going to get quicker." At the same time, Sarah was struggling with the walking and then started to struggle with the running too.

Anyway, we didn't get to the first checkpoint until late and had just 40 minutes before cut off. My feet were sore. Sarah sat out in the sun and sorted her feet instead of getting in the shade. We trekked on. 17 minute miles, head down. Still maintaining it. Then the self-doubt started creeping in, " I can't do this pace, Tony." Sarah was saying, "Run it." I said. "I can't run it, it's too hot." She would say. The pack was rubbing. I was sharing water with her and before we knew it we were down to just one bottle. Then, we took a wrong turn. We genuinely took a wrong turn. We went into a dry river bed where there should have been tape on the left to stop people going left. We went straight over. Obviously, in the winds it had blown away. We followed a couple of other people. Other people said, "Oh we might need your road book." Did you get your map out or follow people, Craig?

Craig - I know what you're saying and I know exactly where you're talking about. Yeah easily done. I remember starting to get down there thinking it's not obvious which way to go there. I often followed others to be fair Tony. I didn't want to get my road book out in the strong winds.

Tony - We went down the river bed for a mile. There was no shade. No breeze. It was brutal, right? Midday sun. Sarah kept saying, "How much further?" I'm going, "It's around the corner." I stopped the 2 people that we followed. I said, "Look guys, we haven't seen a marker and there are no other footprints around us. I climbed about 15 foot up a steep bank and I could make out what I thought was a Jeep.

I climb back and get the girls bags and we crack on towards the Jeep. Eventually we arrived and they told us we have 40 mins before the check point closes. We were 3.8 kilometres away... 2 1/2 miles! You can easily do that on the road, can't you? We set off, but before long Sarah was exhausted, "I need to rest. Just 2 minutes." I go, "We haven't got 2 minutes, we only have 40 minutes do this distance. That's 5% of our time. We haven't got that. We need to crack on!" Probably wasn't the most motivating thing I could have said, but things were starting to slip out of my hands. The pressure got to us and we started arguing. Sarah was pouring water over herself trying to cool herself down. One thing to remember is, don't pour your water over your head. When you get to checkpoints, the faster runners leave half bottles for slower runners to pour over their heads, but you need your water in your body. Again, we ran out of water. That was it. We were timed out.

We came across one of the dot trotters' 4x4's and Sarah climbed in. There was no room for us and I walked to the checkpoint with one of the doctors. That was it, we were out. That's when we came across Mr. Jackson too.

Craig - Ted was there too?

Tony - Ted was timed out too.

Craig – All that must've been tough. I can't imagine how you felt.

Tony - I feel like I've got unfinished business. You know what I mean on this one, don't you?

Craig - Yeah. That's up to you, Tony. I remember I posted a little video, you messaged me and you were like, 'it's in your head.' You sent me a picture of your feet and I was like, "Jeeze!" You were just like, "Get it right in your head. You'll do this."

Tony - I do say that. I believe success in the MDS is 20, 20, 20, 40. Your food, your kit, your fitness, and then your head in those percentages and in that order.

Craig - I know from my survey. People see it more like 50% fitness, 20% kit, 20% food, 10% in your head. Well I am sure with this interview and the rest of this book we can get people to flip that to what you said, 20, 20, 20 & 40!

Thanks Tony, it's been great chatting to you and getting the benefit of your experience.

CHAPTER 19

INTERVIEW WITH
PHIL KELLY

Performance Coach To Athletes, High Level Excutives And Entreprenuers

Phil Kelly is a coach with an uncanny ability to clarify things, and to dig deep into the way and how of your thoughts. In other parts of this book I talk about and chat to his business partner Phil Quirk who leads Hbp-Nlp.com, the mindset half of their rapidly growing business and Phil Kelly leads the Hbp-Training.com side. HBP-Training focus on human behaviour and performance. What human factors or behaviour caused the death of a worker in an industrial accident perhaps? Or... most recently... what human factors and behaviour led to a loss of millions on the stock exchange.

Craig – Hi Phil, I have been looking forward to this chat for a while now and just wondered what behaviour led to you delaying it for so long?

Phil – That's a great question Craig, but what proof do you have that your jokes are funny?

Craig – Err... fuck... you've got me already (laughs). Seriously though Phil, I truly look forward to every time we speak. I always get so much clarity of thought and a deeper understanding of why human do what humans do... or don't do in some cases. Can you give the readers an insight into what it is you do or have been doing recently? It'll add a little authority to what you're saying and increase the impact.

Phil – Ok, let me frame it this way... 2016, coming into 2017... fibre optic internet, instant information constantly plugged in to social media and receiving info. What an amazing age, but when talking to everyone from my next-door neighbour, to CEOs of business & professional athletes, we are completely overwhelmed. Some of the information we need, some of it, we don't. We can call it what we want, an addiction to information, an addiction to mobile phones, we can call it addiction to social media, but the result is the same. It's a complete overload of information. Now trying to make sense of it all causes some problems.

Effectively, what I've found myself doing lately, certainly for the last six or seven months, is sitting down with individuals, teams, organizations, and just taking that time out asking good, pointed questions. Very exploration based questions, in terms of, "What is actually going on around you right now? What is the current situation?" People often try and work too far in advance.

I suppose in many ways, I'm a performance coach, I'm a clarity coach, but what I do in basic terms, I just find out what's going on, in and around people? I increase their level of situational awareness? How are things intertwined between what's going on in the organization or the teams? I work in organizational performance and individual performance, and personal development.

Craig - Good, Phil I want to concentrate on a couple of things in this interview. Overwhelm and self-induced pressure are huge factors in the reader's preparation for the MDS or any other challenging event, so let's chat about how we can prevent it, eradicate it or maybe even use it during our prep and during the event itself. I know the brain is always processing information and it must generalise, distort, and delete much of what we receive through our vision, hearing, touch, smell and taste so how do you think what our modern brain is doing and how does the natural processes we are constantly running affect overwhelm and self-induced pressure?

Phil - Well, the brain's amazing. Depending on what we choose to focus on will flood our unconscious & subconscious brain with information, and then, somehow, we've got to gain some sort of alignment between the two of them so that it makes sense to us. Sense-making is difficult now, for most people because we live fast-paced lives. We're up early in the morning, we're rushing to get the kids to school, we're rushing to get the packed lunch together, we're packing kids into the car, we're picking them up after school. Oh, and it's not 9-5 anymore, it's six 'til ten, and two 'til six, maybe even seven o'clock. We're not really finding a natural rhythm for ourselves to get into the habits that we like as human beings. What most people do to gain some clarity is use conversation. Chat to close family and friends, they'll discuss things with them and in talking, find clarity, but sometimes what happens with family and friends is, with all the best intentions, they muddy the waters even more, or they tell them what they 'should' be doing. They add an extra layer of complexity.

Now your brain has the answers and can sift through everything when used in the right way or when given enough time without distraction. There's too many things going on. It's everything from, like I said, things that go on in the traffic, we'll have the phone going, we'll have the radio on, we'll be thinking in our head of the meeting we need to go to when we get to work. We're wondering about what's going to happen in the afternoon, and then the basic stuff we need as human beings, such as food and water, they become an afterthought. We just stumble into lunch... jeeze where did that come from... I'll grab it at some point.

Craig - Yeah, we've kind of become reactive to everything and ultimately get pushed around or smothered.

Phil – Yeah and taking care of yourself as well. Going for a run and getting some fresh air, having some reset moments. It doesn't have to be something as advanced as what you've done Craig, because I think your MDS was a massive reset exercise for you? To go out, push yourself, get to the point where you are physically exhausted, fatigue, hurting, hungry and thirsty, when you just go into autopilot. All you can do is put one foot in front of the other. In that moment of desperation comes clarity, because on the grand scheme of things. Much of the other stuff we stress about feels important, but after that... you gain new perspective.

In times like that small stuff become the big stuff and you must have a handle on it. You know you've got food, water is taken care of, I know where my next checkpoint is, all you must do is keep on moving. Then... "Hey, life's not so bad, we make it hectic, get rid of all the crap, let's go back to basics and start rebuilding it."

Craig - Yeah. When you start thinking about the athletes and the people that you work with them, how often do you identify overwhelm, or self-induced pressure as root causes to friction in their preparation? The two are different I suppose, aren't they? There's overwhelm, we can be overwhelmed by lots of different stuff, but then self-induced pressure, this is something that we pile on ourselves, so let's separate the two. How often do you come across people that are just overwhelmed?

Phil - Quite often. It's not the most dominant factor, but it basically boils down to a lack of clarity, rabbit in the head light type thing. I'm working with some athletes now that, they're overwhelmed in terms of the stage of their life. They're young professionals, their early 20's, they're still in university, as well, so they've got all their university new friends they want to keep on board, so you've got the social aspect of that. They've got the pressure of family and friends that want to see them get on and kick on with their professional careers. Their sport is high profile at the moment, it's in the news most days, so that adds more pressure, plus the life changes of somebody late teens, early 20's going on.

It's massively overwhelming, so the first thing we need is a bench mark to help us make decisions and ultimately act. We start with a list of priorities, in terms of what's most important right now. Once you've got a list of priorities, your decision making becomes easier. Now you can justify it to yourself and we gain clarity.

Other athletes, based around fast-based sports, where split-second decisions make the difference between success and failure. It's not the overwhelm, in terms of the occasion, it's the level of self-awareness, understanding why sometimes they behave in a way that decreases their chances of winning rather than increases. One of the professional cyclists I was working with in the last couple of weeks excelled in the last 12 months, but he makes strange decisions in the heat of a race. It comes back to the three F's, skills we developed as primitive beings... which is the fight, flight, and freeze (or in the correct order freeze, flight or fight). They get a little bit threatened by somebody that may knock them off their bike, so it's the fear of losing, getting knocked off the bike and injured, the fear of losing the momentum that, then, the flight kicks in and they drive hard through the pedals, kick off on the bike, and they'll put a lot of effort and energy to get away from that situation. Great a few K from the finish line, but not great too early in the race.

Once we started discovering what's important a whole new range of options become available. For example, making sure the team protects them a little bit more, maybe riding at the front of the group, maybe riding to the outside, maybe ensure you have an experienced rider alongside you. The ability to be proactive with what's going on, rather than reactive.

Craig – Phil – So let's bring this a little more in line with the MDS. Obviously, you know all about MDS, you were there during my prep, and we had loads of chats about it. Have you got any nuggets of information that could help these people that are in this situation, whether getting ready for this massive event, potentially something they've dreamed of doing for years and years, and they're just paralyzed by the 'facts' or by what others are doing?

Phil - Yeah, I've got a very simple tool I use

with a lot of my clients if we just need to grease the wheels, on their thought process. It's the traffic light system, red, amber, green. Red - Stop the things that are harming your progress. What factors are you concerned about that you can do nothing about or will have very little effect on your preparation. Amber - Start something. What do you need to start to prepare better today than you did yesterday? That's how momentum is built... small steps each day aiming to be a little better than you were. Finally, Green – Continue, what are we doing well, what positives should we continue doing and I suggest there is ALWAYS something we are doing well. It may not be huge, we just need to recognize some wins and build on them. The most common 'Stop' I come across is our innate need to compare ourselves to everybody else.

Let's look at the effect of comparing yourself to others. Look at them, look how big and strong and fast they are. Look at the time they 'appear' to be doing in training. Look at them on Facebook going out for another run, they have all their kit and food sorted already. They manage to do 15 miles a day in their runs. Now look at me... I can't do that because I've got a wife and kids at home, and a business to run. This thinking is flawed on so many levels. You're comparing yourself, potentially against a) somebody who's professional, but certainly somebody who's in a different situation to you.

It may be somebody that's amateur who's got professional sponsorship, so they've got that three or four months to dedicate to prep. When we worry about things we have got no control over, it has a damning impact on our personal performance as an individual. They may be looking at the kit they've got, they may be looking at past race times, they're looking at what they don't want, "I don't want to be last, I don't want to drop out." When if you bring it back to a structured plan, and working day-to-day to make yourself, the best version of you, within the factors of your life, then that's where you get clarity and momentum. You get belief in what you are preparing for. Often this is where humans are amazing, when you work methodically through a strategic process, we end up overachieving. You just get into a rhythm because everything is just free.

So, every time you catch yourself looking at what others are doing, which I suggest will be daily now, think internally. Look inside... red, amber green and get going again. Get peers who have a similar ability around you and maybe co-train or bounce ideas off each other, but let them compare themselves to you. I want to talk about how you can be truly committed to your decisions shortly, but before that...

Focus your mindset on things that will happen. Focus on the things that you want to become true. What's realistic in my situation. Let's start being positive in my internal dialogue, my language I speak to myself. That will manufacture itself into positive behaviour anyway. Also, the continue would be personal to everybody. People often take the things we are good at for granted, so think of your strengths, remember them, bring it into our conscious awareness. That way we're more likely to do it again and repeat it and confidence is like a muscle too. The more we use it the more we get.

Craig - Yeah. Obviously, as always when I talk to you, loads of stuff just fill my head. When you said, "Think about continuing to do the things that you know you're really good at." Immediately my mind snapped to downhills. I know I'm very brave running downhill. It's a small thing, but I know that when we get to downhills, I can just power down there and can quickly make distance up. Other people start slowly picking their way down the hill, and it's something I used on the MDS a lot. Every time we got to the top, one of the big jebels or sand dunes, I'd just be like, "Right, this is my territory now." I didn't necessarily have the ...

Phil - Why are you good at it?

Craig - I don't really know why I'm good at it. I just remember always being brave downhill, whenever we did a challenge in the marines. I just kind of knew that I was better at that than most. I was just brave in the hills when it was dark and everyone else was fumbling through, and I was like, "Nope, I've got confidence in this," and away I'd go.

I guess I had a history of doing it in the past and doing well at it.

Phil - You had past successes? Okay. So how often was that and how long ago was that?

Craig - Years. I mean... Every time we did a navigational exercise at night or something like that, I just found this to be true, so at least every couple of months we'd do something where you just need a bit of bravery at night time on rough terrain, and I'd fly along.

Phil - I don't know if you thought about it before, but that's the way you hook into your internal belief system. You've done it in the past, you've got success, you've done it more than once, so your brain knows you can do it. Now, when you have to pull that back, confidence is directly linked to it.

Now we can only experience something for the first time once and too often, when we have a new experience, or a new process, we fail to attribute a positive emotion to it. Our subconscious mind stores every experience we have ever had as a form of reference so we know how to act when we end up in the same situation.

If we don't manage to link a positive emotion to the event we can create a belief that we're not that good at it. This can then strengthen as our initially belief looks for evidence to support the belief. 'See... I told you I wasn't good at that!" but we can change these beliefs. We all believed at one time that we were 4. We knew this to be 100% true, but now we believe we are older and we now know this to be true.

Craig - Yeah, and I suppose there's people that'll be reading this, and they'll be a handful that's hardly run before, but I daresay, if you're going to tackle the MDS, you've done something already, you know what I mean? It's not often the first event like this that you just crack. They'll have a history of doing all sorts... running, covering similar distances, experiencing similar heat, so I'm sure there's confidence for everyone to find, isn't there?

Phil - Yeah, there's got to be a logical process in terms of, there's been over optimistic so... 'I haven't done a half marathon or 10k run before, but I'm going to enter the MDS and I'm going to do it with no training'. Logically, you know that's not correct, but even if it is... you have time now to gradually increase your confidence with events prior to the MDS.

You're going to get a little knock back, you might get an injury, you might have issues with work for a few days. Let's look at that as an example. So, you must have a break from your training programme because of work. You could get in a tizz because your progress has been affected, but this can crush our motivation. When we focus on the things we cannot change we become static. How about reframing the situation? 'I've got to go away three or four days and I can't train, so I will refrain this as a rest phase, and then I'm going to go a little bit harder and a little bit quicker when I come back. I will have had a good rest, so I'll be fresh." Now we are using the situation rather than the situation abusing us.

Craig - It's funny. Elsewhere in this book, I talk about a presentation I heard from Dr Mike Stroud during the MDS Expo. Thinking about what we are good at, you might struggle to think of something, but actually you look at our anatomy and how we evolved. We are born to run across distances and terrain like this. Our bodies have adapted to be very good at dissipating heat, so I think everybody can take confidence in the fact that this is what we were born to do. We've kind of forgotten how to do it, or lost confidence in our ability to do it. You know what I mean? We sit behind desks, and we drive cars and all that now, but if we shake out the cobwebs, we were born for this.

Phil – Well when you consider the basics of us, we shouldn't be on this planet, really! We're not the biggest, we're not the hardest, we're not the fastest, we don't have the biggest teeth, we're not the scariest, but for good reason, we've been able to evolve and learn exceptionally quickly how to survive. That's our cognitive ability to make decisions, whether quickly learning through other people's failings. That massive lizard... that's got really bad eyesight, so when it's around we need to freeze.

"Oh, that little scary animal over there, it's not that quick, it's quite clumsy, we can run away from that." We very rarely must engage the fight syndrome to be honest, but it seems we often end up fighting our emotions and our external verifications when comparing ourselves to others.

Craig - Yeah. When I surveyed some MDS runners, it uncovered loads of different stuff that they were worried about, their biggest fears that were contributing to being stuck right now. I'm just going to throw a couple of them out, and then see what your take is on this.

Phil – A bit of a prediction before we start, but I can guess that there will be a fear of no knowledge, so they will be questions around kits, timings, distance, first aid, which are practical. Then there will be the secondary ones then, "What if I'm left behind? What if I need to evacuate? What's this? What's that?", but I am interested and looking forward to it because there might be some left field ones.

Craig – Ok, the biggest one was the fear that I'm not fit enough.

Phil - Yeah. What's that mean?

Craig - Yeah, well, exactly. You picked up on the word 'enough'. It's like... what's fit enough? What does enough actually mean? For me, I just wanted to go and experience it. I knew that, deep down, regardless of how fast I completed it, I had it in me to go and do it. Like you said, I surpassed my own expectations by just taking it bit by bit. When I got back I had overachieved, compared to what I expected to do. There's a lot of hype around the event and don't get me wrong you must respect it. They called it the toughest foot race on earth for a reason.

Phil - Yeah for sure. I ... Sorry Craig, your first statement there, in terms of, "I'm concerned I'll not be quick enough." Well, what is quick enough? What is your target? Where is that coming from? What's the information feeding into that? Is that realistic? There's so many more questions in and around that to extract information. Who's driving that? Is that coming from yourself? Is it because you think other people think that of you? Is that what people are expecting? All of them, can be realigned. Maybe a little bit of situational awareness again, and understanding what's going on. Also, just having coaching conversation, we can clear that up by defining what 'fit enough' means, because right now it means nothing! It's just a fuzzy thought in your head.

Craig - Yeah.

Phil - Yeah, so if it were somebody saying, "I'm really concerned I'm not going to finish," then that's fine, you can have a really good conversation in and around that.

Craig - In what respect?

Phil - Well, if someone is concerned they're not going to finish, then that's a little clearer for me. Sometimes that's easier to work with. When somebody says, "I'm not sure I'm fit enough," it's a bit of a blasé statement, so I need to work with them to get a specific point, and then we can go in and set some goals in that. Some specifics.

Craig - Yeah, cool. That's gold dust. The next one is fear of injury.

Which is a common one. I remember a couple of weeks out, I was petrified of getting a common cold, to the point where I was restricting who I talked to and if somebody coughed, I'd freak out. You must experience that as some of your athletes and that get ready for major competitions.

Phil - Look at your response though. That's

positive. You're aware that you've committed a lot of time, money and emotions into your preparation. You're aware of that, potentially towards the end of your training program you're at your most vulnerable. Therefore, you are going to pick up little coughs and your right to be cautious. Being aware of what's going on around you and making those decisions like, "Right, is there a potential warning sign over there with someone coughing, I'm going to go over here."

You're taking everything you can in your circle of influence, you're taking positive steps. Socially, that might be awkward, but at that moment in time, what's more important? Is protecting your health for the race that you've committed yourself for a year, two years in training, or maybe just go in saying it, "I know it's important that the conversation here, but I'm sensing a bit of a cold. That's the last thing I need. I'm flying out in a week's time, so don't think I'm being ignorant." You're taking control of the situation then. I know professional athletes that, granted it's a different world, but they only get private jets. They want to avoid germs circulated in air conditioning. So, let's pull it back... what can you do? Can you make sure you are getting sufficient rest? Can you talk to the family around you about the importance of staying healthy? Is your diet sufficient to ensure you're taking your vitamins in?

Craig - All right. Brilliant, again. Injuries are a definite worry, but I think what I take from what you said is, really focus on the circles of influence.

If it happens, react positively. If it doesn't happen, brilliant, but there's no point worrying.

Phil - Yeah, definitely.

Craig - The next one was kit. People completely obsess over having the right kit.

Phil - I suppose here's a question back to you, I've not done the MDS, so, how vital was it for you to have the right kit, and how much research did you do beforehand? Obviously, I classed you, Craig, as a great success story of the MDS. You know, you were strong, you finished much quicker than you wanted to, you were healthy. Obviously, you had your ups and downs, which no doubt you talk about in the rest of the book, but how vital was it to you?

Craig - There were some things that are vital, but there's also a lot of stuff that people took that they didn't really need. I think I was quite lucky that I'd had a good few years in the marines, where I learned the benefit of learning the importance of not duplicating kit. Why take a knife, fork, spoon, when a spoon will do, you know? I don't really know of anybody that failed because they didn't have the right kit. Yeah, to be comfortable and to get the job done, that's probably about 20% of the whole thing.

Phil - Yeah. Would it be fair to say, then, Craig, if you've done your research and you've experimented a little throughout your training cycle to make the best decision you possibly can, there's not a lot you can do about that? Especially when you are stood on the start line.

Craig - No, there's not a lot you can do. Actually, at the end of the day, people used to do this in standard running shoes and a little military backpack, some sandwiches on their back, and off they went. They didn't have this super light-weight clothing, UV protection shirts and energy gels.

Phil – Yes, it's phenomenal, like the first project we worked together on, the South Pole expedition. Everybody's got on £300, £400, £500 GORE-TEX jackets and £300 walking boots, but then when you look at what the originals did it in, it's phenomenal what humans are capable of. I think it really links nicely to what you were saying... as human beings, we've evolved well, but I also think we've gone backwards a few steps in terms of losing touch of what our biggest strengths are and what we're really capable of overcoming. We take a lot of things for granted in our daily life and that's what feeds into overwhelm, as well, I think. When you've got a standard expectation of x, y, and z, but you only get x and y, that can create a frustration, when actually, z is not important.

Craig - I think what I've just realized there is that, for me, it was quite easy to live with next to no kit, but what if you've got somebody that has not really lived like that before, possibly never even been camping in their life? You've got smart phones, the house packed full of gadgets, and kit to make life easy. To strip a lot of that back can be a little bit scary and I can understand why people obsess over the kit.

I think it's easy to forget that as human beings, what we're talking about here with kit is resources, but it's not a case of not having enough resources, it's not having enough resourcefulness. We can always improvise and overcome. We've done that all through evolution, and that's how we probably got to here. Sometimes we forget we've got this inbuilt ability to improvise, and just get through stuff. If we need to make a bloody bowl out of an empty water bottle, then we will do it. On the MDS, one of the guys broke his spoon, so I cut a water bottle up and made a little spoon for him. You always get through.

Phil - It's just phenomenal what we're capable of. It's amazing to think about it. If everybody reading your book and listening to these articles is ... If you really thought about that one time you were really up against it, and you've come through, that moment of inspiration, you always remember that.

I told the story on my Ted Talk where I was released from a professional football club at an early age. It had always been my dream to be a pro footballer and I never thought I would do anything else. By rights I should have been sulking and kicking off as the boss sat in his massive leather chair saying, "Sorry fellow, we're going to have to let you go." Inside... my whole world was falling apart. My personal values took over and I found the resources to go over and thank him for his effort and shook his hand. I went around the stadium thanking all the personal assistants and the youth coaches. While I was saying, "I really appreciated all your help." Other lads were storming outside slamming the door, and I was wondering, "Why am I so different? What is it?" I think it's that word resourcefulness. I was frustrated after, and I was obviously bitter and angry, because naturally, we are all human beings and emotions do play a part in our lives, or else life would be bloody boring, wouldn't it?

When we're up against it, I think if we really have a good level of self-awareness, we can come across, or certainly perform at an ability that's aligned of our natural personality. Through that comes creativity and resourcefulness.

Craig - Brilliant. Next biggest worry was food. Getting food right and making sure they've got enough food.

Phil - What was your experience there? Was people quite calculated, or was it just that they didn't know their body enough to understand what they needed?

Craig - It was over calculated, but not based on a great deal of science. People kind of guessed how many calories per day they would need, then obsessed over getting the figures right. Most it was sugar, and in this book, we talk about running on fats. Loads of people were sucked into these commercial food companies.

Sugar isn't good for your emotions either, because you get peaks and troughs with your energy levels, and that gives you peaks and troughs with your emotions. I see it at our fitness camp all the time. When you start to run on fat, you're just a lot more level headed and can make better decisions. You can sustain activity for much longer. It's just a lot better.

Phil - Yeah. The short-term solution is there. It'll mask over the cracks on it, so when you're doing something like the MDS, which is purely endurance, those cracks can get wider and wider, and then suddenly, there's a huge one and you fall through it and you wonder why.

Craig – Speaking of resources... another thing is we often forget that every one of us, even the leanest person, has got enough calories to get through the MDS without eating anything. We wouldn't want to because it would be detrimental to our health, but we could. We've got enough resources and enough reserves. The first two or three days of the 2016 race, I estimate I was only eating about 700 calories, which is a third of what you're expected to eat. I still did ok.

Phil - Why was that, because you didn't want to eat? You couldn't eat, or was that part of your plan?

Craig - I just didn't have an appetite. I think it was a combination of the exertion and heat.

Phil - Yeah, of course. Then, you were working to a plan, weren't you? Which is obviously vital. Plans change. There's two sides of planning for me, there's the strategic planning, like, "I'm going for this amount a day and covering this distance. This is how many calories I'm going to burn each day, this is what I need to eat."

You must have dealt with that well then Craig?

You surely didn't plan that tactically, but you come to terms with that it quickly?

Craig - Yeah, I come to terms with quite a lot after the first leg. The desert basically put me over its knee and slapped my ass, and said, "You will fucking respect me a little bit." I had to make a couple of changes to my plan. Straight away I thought, "Right, I will not even try to run on soft uphill or flat sand," whereas in my preparation I was thinking, I'll run the downhill and run the flats. I didn't have the fitness levels to be running on the flats in the soft sand, so I made the decision I wasn't going to try that anymore.

I also made the decision that I would start my recovery long before I even got back to the bivouac, with regards to food and water. A couple of k from the end, I would start drinking my recovery shake and start eating a bit of food. I wanted to be in a better state when I got back instead of depleting everything to get to the finish line and then just struggling with it all. Yeah, there was loads of little decisions I made tactically as the plan changed.

Craig - Cool. Phil, that's about 40 minutes now, we've been banging on for. Thanks for your input. Have you got anything else that you think people preparing for an event like this would benefit from?

Phil – Yeah. One thing that I've used with a lot of my private clients and professional athletes is using Cartesian logic. Not just to gain under-standing of what's going on now, but also to create planning for the future. Let's take an example of your equipment. You were saying there's people have a bit of angst about, 'How much kit do I take?', 'How much food do I take?'

I think Cartesian logic which maybe you'll be able to put a diagram into the book, is asking 4 questions from different angles.

1. What will happen if I do take it?
2. What will happen if I don't take it?
3. What won't happen if I do take it?
4. What won't happen if I don't take it?

(See the Cartesian logic video & diagram at RunningLightBook.com/Resources)

What that gets you to do is really think around the problem you have at hand, and then you'll very soon be able to make a really, strong, well informed decision. A decision you can feel assured you have justified to yourself.

Once you make an informed decision you stop having regrets. Even if it doesn't work out right. You've made the best decision with the information available, so if the situations change, you just have to make another decision. That'll detach emotions from your decisions. It's the emotions that drain you. It's the frustration, the anger, the fear. That's what really drains your batteries and your resources.

Using that has paid dividends in the past. The people that have filled it in have really bought in to their decision and gone full throttle through the acts they need to take based off that decision.

Craig - I think that's just summarized the whole of this perfectly. At the end of the day, people are worried, they've got angst, they're paralyzed by all their analysis, and why? Because basically, they just want to make the right decision, but they are not understanding that every decision is the right decision. There's so many ways to skin this cat, and there's so many ways to get this right. A couple of years ago, a guy did it with an ironing board strapped to his back. Years gone by, they've done it with sandwiches in a little knapsack. Trust that you've got all the resources you need and you've just got to make the right decision, but it's the right decision for you. I think Cartesian logic is going to be a good exercise when they start drilling down into some of the decisions they need to make.

Phil - Yeah, that's the short end of decision making. The other one is, you need to have a focal point or refocusing point. If something is not going right, you need something to return to. A safe place. If you fully understand the reasons why:

a) you want to do the marathon to start, and

b) you made the decisions you have made you can break through paralysis.

If you have that core central theme aligned, you know, "Why am I doing this? Have I really thought this through?" Then once you've got that, everything else will be easy because you'll be able to refer to that, so when things are not going right, and a few decisions are wrong, just reflect on the reasons why you're there, and that'll give you a moral compass to make your future decisions.

Craig - Yeah, it's funny because before we got on this call I was writing about creating a big reason why. When your reason is strong enough, the facts don't matter. You'll conquer anything.

Brilliant, Phil. Thanks for your time and how can people learn more about you or even get a little of your Cartesian

If you want to learn more about Phil Quirk & Phil Kelly, then you can find him on Facebook, HBP-NLP or HBP Training. They're two slightly different angles to this business, or you can go to his website, hbp-training.com.

CHAPTER 20

MY **RACE DIARY**

April 2016 - Arrival Day

Just looking out of the window as we start our final descent into Morocco. The terrain is intimidating to say the least. I can see some of the large sand dunes and immediately I wonder if they're the fuckers we will be trekking over soon enough. I sat next to a guy called Lee Roy on the plane. We chatted a little, turns out he only started running 12 months ago. He seemed calm and relaxed. 'It seems like there is no need or if fact room for complexity here' said Lee Roy. 'I have just kept things really simple and not tried to overthink everything.' Great line and a great way to address what you could make way to complicated. After all, it's just you and the desert for a week!

The flight was pretty smooth albeit brimming with nervous energy. What strikes me immediately was the huge mix of people. There were lots of serious looking runners as well as lots of serious runners. Experience has repeatedly shown that people that look don't always perform as good as they look. It would have been easy to pile extra pressure on myself there and then and I wondered how many other 'have-a-go', average runners like me were getting psyched out by people with all the gear.

Arriving in Morocco for the MDS is centred around a huge coach journey with what seemed like 20 coaches all lined up. The atmosphere is brilliant! It was evident immediately that this was a slick operation too. Okay there was a little hanging around and queuing, but we were flying in to a foreign country so that was to be expected.

If I hadn't felt part of the MDS at Gatwick I certainly did when I stepped out of the Moroccan airport to a bank of eager race marshals and the man himself... the nut job that dreamed up this event, Patrick Bauer! He had a hand shake and a kiss for everyone! It felt a little err... 'French' for me. I don't even hug my mum often and take offence sometimes if my wife asks for a hug. I didn't spend over 13 years having my emotions systematically removed by the Marines to get snogged by a middle-aged guy dressed like Steve Irwin. Nevertheless, I went with it and as Patrick tried to neck on with each of us, the race marshals cheered and sang songs. It was a little bit of effort on the event organisers part, but it made the arrival memorable.

Welcome to the MDS...

I just collected a pack lunch and climbed on to the coach with the lads that would end up being my tent mates for the duration. Though most of us are dressed in shorts, t-shirts or other summer attire, a fella called Pete is dressed in a white snake skin jacket. A bit bizarre, but it takes all sorts I suppose.

Great bread! I avoid bread usually and wonder if it's going to block me up and make me bloat for a while. No point worrying. I need the food.

I'm sat next to Mark on the coach. We met through a mutual friend at the MDS Expo. Mark described how he had injured himself during training and was a little devastated with not being able to prepare as he wanted. Mark completed the MDS 2 years prior and had a wealth of marathon experience. The excitement and nervousness reminds me of deploying on operations in the forces.

The MDS is famous for many things and I wonder if it also holds the record for the longest line of foreign nationals pissing at the side of the road. We stopped mid-way through the coach trip to have lunch and check out each other's knobs. The ladies joined in too, which was nice! Mark explained that this is a sign of things to come with regards to urinating (as well as other stuff!) during the race.

My tips here would be:

Think hygiene from the minute you get on the plane to prevent the shits etc.

Stay in the shade. Lots of runners, who obviously weren't the white skinned fair hairs Saxon that I am were worshipping the sun as soon as they got in country. I have seen many soldiers come a cropper with this.

Relax. There's potential to burn through a lot of nervous energy during this stage.

Eventually we arrived at the Bivouac and found a tent that we would call home for the week. I settled into the middle area with Paul to my right and snakeskin Pete to my left. We have some great guys, Mark from the coach journey, Pete, me, Paul, Si, Euan and another Mark. I wasn't the only ex-service man as Euan had served in the guards and Mark No#2 had huge experience in the Royal Military Police.

Day 1 - Admin Day

Very relaxed start to the day after what began as a beautiful, clear night with the immense stars you can only see with minimal light pollution. I was lucky enough laid in the centre of the tent to be able to look directly up to the stars and watched a few shooting stars for a while.

I don't remember drifting off to sleep, but it must have been peaceful. Well until I was woken suddenly with a powerful sand storm. I thought the tent would take off as one point and sand seemed to blow into every bit of my kit. I pulled the draw cord on my sleeping bag as tight as it would go and drifted in and out of sleep for a while. I remember the sand storm dying down a little, but a sudden drop in temperature followed. I had chosen an OMM sleeping bag which I realise now stands for 'Ommm... I made the wrong choice!' I was cold in the night, but fortunately the silk sleeping bag liner afforded me a little extra comfort.

Kit check and registration was relatively painless. Again, though there was a little waiting and queuing. Everyone knew what they had to do and when and 30 odd years of running this thing was evident.

I had a couple of texts from home. I checked my phone every now and then before checking it in with my luggage. I won't see it again now until the end, but the texts were a huge boost. My biggest reason for doing the MDS was to inspire others and to know my wife was so proud gave me a sudden surge of energy.

The night before...

I don't really feel intimidated yet. Still excited. There is a great atmosphere in the Bivouac area. I had a very rare can of coke. I haven't drunk coke for years and have worked hard to break free of sugars like this during training. It tasted way too sweet to me, but I savoured it, knowing I had some hardship approaching. I'm actually in bed way too early, but most people are keen for tomorrow to arrive and are also in their time accelerators. I'm starting the night with my liner in the sleeping bag tonight. Don't want to get caught out in the early hours of the night again.

Patrick Bauer briefed us all on the race at around 1600. The sun was still beating down and the heat generated thoughts of the fun we would have in the sand dunes tomorrow.

I have helped a few people with taping their feet. It seems I am known as either 'the blister guy' of the 'YouTube guy'. My sons Danny & matt will be so proud... of the latter not the former. They'll think that's plain weird!

I have just finished taping my feet and now it's time to rest. Tomorrow it all begins...

Stage 1

Wow!!! That was tough. The sand dunes were pretty brutal at times though achievable. The wind made it even more challenging. We faced a constant head on sand storm. I was quite dehydrated and could feel the onset of heat exhaustion at check point 1, about 12 km in. I managed to avoid the need for medical treatment after setting off way too fast but...

The scenery was immense. The colours of the sand were so varied and I think I have seen every shade of sand already. I saw loads of little scarab beetles and lizards and even a black camel. I never knew they excised!

The race crew are amazing as are the doc trotters, though very keen to drip me up!

Highlights include:

- Dunes - Very tough, but reminiscent of the desert scene in Star Wars

- Heat illness!!!

- Potentially out of the race at C.P. 1 because I went to quick at the start. Pete told me to get out of the 'spaz tent!'

- Wind - Was head on and constant

- Webcam - I spent a few moments blowing kisses to Paula and waving to my family and friends on the webcam. I wonder if they can see me.

Right now, I am telling myself to take it all in and enjoy it. All thugs and anything else that happens is my choice!

Also... knowing people can track you along the route is incredibly motivating.

Stage 2

Devastating day today. We have lost 2 people from our tent and they lost 4 from next door. Throughout the whole day there were countless people being airlifted to safety due to heat issues. The terrain is as unforgiving as the restriction to water and is beaten only by the relentless heat. The previous MDS veteran Mark and Euan. Euan turned an ankle which was all too easy in the terrain. He was in pain physically, but was also upset to be out the race. Mark had stopped for a short 5 min nap and work up in the helicopter on a drip being evacuated. He would eventually have 6 bags of fluid, which Pete described simply as 'kidney failure territory!' Feck... this shit is very real!!!

But...

Personally, I had a much better day. I felt much stronger and was motivated by not wanting to spend any longer than I had to out in the desert. Stay with the bow wave! I did have a slightly dodger moment at C.P. 3. I gave myself 10 mins to hydrate and get a little extra food on board. I made a very smart choice of packing my recovery shake in my front pouch and decided I would drink some of it if my blood sugar levels dropped too low.

Commando training and countless deployments to the desert are so valuable to me. It's funny how 'context' can change your perspective of things. Previously I struggled with my operations in Iraq and Afghan, but now... during the MDS I was eternally grateful for the experience. It gave me the presence of mind to manage water and food properly.

I was asked today how this compared to Commando Training - It doesn't!!!

Euan has just returned from the tent on crutches with a heavily bandaged ankle. That's a shame and could have happened to anyone of us. Euan shared a combat assessment process with the tent called the OODA loop. Story has it that the fastest jet pilots in dog fights over Korean into the OODA loop survived the longest. I thought it would be worth explaining it here as a strategy during crisis.

- Observe
- Orientate
- Decide
- Act

It's a simple reminder to help you make the best decision you can in stressful times such as heavy gunfire during combat and even caught in the MDS shitter when your toilet roll blows away!!! Trust me... I know!

Anyone out of the race must surrender their food immediately. Mark explained it was for two fundamental reasons. The first is reduce the chance of you sharing it with your tent mates and secondly so you don't return to the desert after being evacuated to attempt to complete the course on your own. Mark and Euan booth dined in the huge dining tent that night and Mark managed to smuggle a can of coke out for us to share. Heaven!!! It tasted very good after 2 days in the dunes.

I got some great emails from Paula and a few others. They make such a huge difference. It's incredible how messages from home can completely eradicate any negative thoughts and feelings I am feeling right now.

I have started breaking the day down into 3 phases:

1. Easy out - A reminder that getting carried away at the start can have serious repercussions

2. Play for position - Progressively pick off the super quick starters that are starting to suffer and make my way up through the field of runners.

3. Live for another day - Ease back on the pace and start recovery and hydration.

Stage 3

Complete! Though not without problems. I vomited blood after completing the stage today. I had a bit of nausea at the end of each day, but today was different and the sight of the blood worried me. I had another incredible insight into the power of the mind today. I have just returned from the medical tent. I was so close to going for a check-up, but as I stood in the doorway of the medical tent the notice boards by race control caught my attention. They had posted the results from the last few days. Somehow, I found the strength to walk across and check them. It took me about ten mins to find my name. I was 425th!!! Is that right? I cannot believe I am much higher in the rankings than I thought possible! Crazy thing was - I didn't go for medical help. I'll keep going and take my chance with Dr Death (Pete).

The stage was challenging with 12k of sand dunes on one leg. I was a little slower today in prep for the biiiiiig stage tomorrow. I am concentrating on reducing time in the check points today. Quite a few people are moving over the sand much quicker than me, but I seem to get in and out of the check point before them. 'Let's walk up the hill and shag all the cows!'

We had to climb a huge jebel at the halfway point today which I really motored up. I prepared well for it with a homemade peanut bar from Tony and his girlfriend Sarah. I'm gutted they are out, but they peanut bar was awesome. I washed it down with plenty of water, an extra salt tablet and some electrolyte drink before I made the steep climb.

My feet were sore today. I have stripped all the tape off to inspect them and allow them to air overnight. Despite a little bruising and the missing toenails, they are in good shape considering.

(2 hours later) We're all back and I think all of us in our tent feel better today. Pete reassured me that the blood is more than likely nothing to worry about and probably due to heavy wrenching with an empty stomach. Big day tomorrow. We all seem to be feeling impending doom, but like every other step... it just needs to be done!

Stage 4 - Long stage - 84k... OMG!!!

Had a couple of 'moments' and the terrain was tough today. It included over 1000m of climbs. One large jebel had ropes to help us scale the steep rocks. Personally, I was good until C.P. 4-5 which never seemed to stop climbing. I had to take a little time out of the midday sun again today, which seems par for the course for me now. The sheer distance was unbelievable and I made the decision to bang it out in one go and not rest or cook en-route. The late 9k were relentless and I even hallucinated at one point and ended up trying to race two land rovers that I thought were other runners trying to flank me in the distance. I could see the bivouac illuminated in the distance, but it just didn't seem to get any closer... ever!!!

Rest day

Not a lot to report today. Just resting and refuelling following the long stage. I cannot believe people are still out on the course. I feel for those that went for the slower strategy today. The sun is relentless. The opening to our tent overlooks the last stage of this leg ... the 9k long 'death march' the finish. I can see the back markers literally limping in to the finish.

Stage 5

Today was the marathon stage and it was actually really tough for me. I started the day very tearful and emotional. The MDS had been a dream of mine for over a decade and I was now so close to completing it. Most people were saying that 'if you finish the long stage, you're pretty much there'. I'm not sure lol.

The heat and terrain has kicked my arse all week and I felt it today. My mental prep and mid race strategies have served me very well up to now, but inadequate fitness is hitting me hard at this point. I just haven't recovered as well as the others. Both Paul and Si posted very quick times today. This race is effectively finished now, but we still have the charity stage to get through to claim our finishes medal.

We had a rock concert and prize giving today. I really admire the top runners that have completed the race incredibly quickly, but was also honoured to have run alongside some of the amazing stories from the race. A father and son combination where the son was the youngest finisher in the history of the race and was only allowed to participate as he had a terminal illness and it was dream to complete it before he passed away. I was also blown away by my Walking With The Wounded team mate and double amputee Duncan Slater who despite not quite making it showed more determination and tenacity than anyone I had ever met. We got another can of coke and I have now settled down for some rest before the charity stage and a chance to reflect on the whole event tomorrow.

Charity Stage

Well we made it! This day was by far the hardest for me. I think most of the natural pain suppressors that the body pumps out have disappeared now. I could feel every blister and friction burn. But...

It was great to walk with my tent mates especially Pete and Si. We were joining for a bout

10k by Si's parents... Not only does he hold the title of most handsome man on the 2016 MDs, but he has the nicest parents too! We must have reeked after a week running the desert :)

Met up with Tony, Ted, Mark and the others that had dropped out in the hotel. It was great to see them and hear their tales. Going to get some rest, lots of food and a couple of beers to finish this event off.

I am a huge believer that all humans need challenge. Without challenge we become depressed... our past becomes bigger than our future and we look back on what we were, not what we are going to be... The MDS has been every bit of the emotional and physical roller-coaster I predicted, but it really has been worth every bit of hard work.

Question is... what now?

BEFORE YOU GO...

Thanks

Thank you for taking the time to read this book and I hope you not only enjoyed it, but found some usable strategies that will help you in the future. I look forward to seeing you at my Running Light presentations and workshops throughout the country.

You can find the dates and details at RunningLightBook.com/events.

Alternatively, if you:

- Are a member of a running club, sports club or other

- Are planning an ultra or similar daft event

- Believe you and the people around you would benefit from a Running Light presentation

- Wish to attend one of the Running Light Workshops

- Or if you would like personal support or coaching from me...

Message me at RunningLightBook.com

Made in the USA
San Bernardino, CA
28 May 2018